Social Issues
in Literature

War in John Knowles's
A Separate Peace

Other Books in the Social Issues in Literature Series:

Social Issues in Literature

War in John Knowles's
A Separate Peace

Dedria Bryfonski, Book Editor

GREENHAVEN PRESS
A part of Gale, Cengage Learning

GALE
CENGAGE Learning

Detroit • New York • San Francisco • New Haven, Conn • Waterville, Maine • London

GALE
CENGAGE Learning™

Christine Nasso, *Publisher*
Elizabeth Des Chenes, *Managing Editor*

© 2011 Greenhaven Press, a part of Gale, Cengage Learning

For more information, contact:
Greenhaven Press
27500 Drake Rd.
Farmington Hills, MI 48331-3535
Or you can visit our Internet site at gale.cengage.com

For product information and technology assistance, contact us at

Gale Customer Support, 1-800-877-4253
For permission to use material from this text or product, submit all requests online at www.cengage.com/permissions

Further permissions questions can be emailed to permissionrequest@cengage.com

Articles in Greenhaven Press anthologies are often edited for length to meet page requirements. In addition, original titles of these works are changed to clearly present the main thesis and to explicitly indicate the author's opinion. Every effort is made to ensure that Greenhaven Press accurately reflects the original intent of the authors. Every effort has been made to trace the owners of copyrighted material.

LIBRARY OF CONGRESS CATALOGING-IN-PUBLICATION DATA

War in John Knowles's A separate peace / Dedria Bryfonski, book editor.
   p. cm. -- (Social issues in literature)
  Includes bibliographical references and index.
  ISBN 978-0-7377-5268-7 (hardcover) -- ISBN 978-0-7377-5269-4 (pbk.)
  1. Knowles, John, 1926-2001. Separate peace. 2. Preparatory school students in literature. 3. Male friendship in literature. 4. War in literature. I. Bryfonski, Dedria.
  PS3561.N68S439 2011
  813'.54--dc22

2010033441

Printed in the United States of America
1 2 3 4 5   15 14 13 12 11

ED004

Contents

Chapter 1: Background on John Knowles

   Robert M. Nelson and Hallman Bell Bryant

   A sense of place is an important aspect of Knowles's fiction, reflecting his thesis that people are shaped by their environment as much as by their heredity. In *A Separate Peace*, he explores the duality of the New England character—a blend of savagery and Protestant restraint.

   John Knowles

   Knowles expresses his admiration for his prep school, Phillips Exeter Academy, and acknowledges the important role it played in shaping his life and successes. He grew up in the coal-mining environment of West Virginia, in a world far less cultured than Exeter. Without the training he received at the academy, Knowles doubts he would have been able to graduate from Yale University and write the novel that would bring him fame, *A Separate Peace*.

   John Knowles

   Knowles writes that *A Separate Peace* grew out of his experiences at Phillips Exeter Academy in the summer of 1943. He recalls that the tranquility of his school setting was overshadowed by the knowledge that he would soon be going off to war. Although the events in the novel do not precisely mirror his own school experience, Knowles says that the book is autobiographical in capturing the emotions he felt at the time.

   Elaine Woo

A *Separate Peace* is often compared with J.D. Salinger's *Catcher in the Rye*. Both are enormously successful first novels dealing with the angst of prep school life. *A Separate Peace* explores the conflict between good and evil within a schoolboy as he comes of age.

Chapter 2: *A Separate Peace* and War

At the beginning of *A Separate Peace*, Gene and Phineas are beguiled by the peace of Devon School and reject the reality of World War II. By the end of the novel, Gene has grown from innocence to adulthood, coming to terms with the reality of the war and also with the presence of evil within his own heart.

Chapter 3: Contemporary Perspectives on War

The events of September 11, 2001, had a profound effect on students. They found it hard to concentrate, and their work habits suffered. Teachers should be compassionate with them.

Introduction

Following his graduation from Yale University in 1949, John Knowles set out to become a writer. He worked as a reporter, drama critic, and freelance writer from 1950 to 1955, spending two years traveling and writing in Italy and France. He wrote a novel, *Descent to Proselito*, while in Europe and had it accepted for publication. On the advice of his literary mentor, Thornton Wilder, who befriended Knowles in Europe, he withdrew the novel from publication and began working on a subject nearer to his own heart. Speaking of *Descent into Proselito*, Wilder wrote, "Everything in this novel lacks intensity. . . . Find a subject which you are absorbed in. . . . Select your next subject from the compelling elements in your life. . . ."

With this advice in mind, Knowles returned to the United States and began work on what was to be his first published and most successful work, *A Separate Peace*. The novel draws upon a time that was indelibly stamped on Knowles as a formative period in his life, a summer session in 1943 at his prep school, Phillips Exeter Academy. At Exeter, Knowles enjoyed the peaceful setting of academics heightened by the looming presence of World War II, a war he anticipated he would soon be fighting in. In the words he gives the novel's narrator, Gene Forrester:

> "Everyone has a moment in history which belongs particularly to him. It is the moment when his emotions achieve their most powerful sway over him, and afterward when you say to this person 'the world today' or 'life' or 'reality' he will assume that you mean this moment, even if it is fifty years past. The world, through his unleashed emotions, imprinted itself upon him, and he carries the stamp of that passing moment forever."

A Separate Peace was, for Knowles, a novel that "wrote itself." "No book can have been easier to get down on paper," Knowles wrote in an article in *Esquire* magazine on the twenty-fifth anniversary of the publication of his first novel. The book was first published in England to almost universal acclaim, and the praise of British reviewers enabled Knowles to find a U.S. publisher. American critics similarly lauded the novel, and *A Separate Peace* became both a classic novel that is part of the high school English curriculum and a cult novel popular with young people. Its popularity and enduring nature are in large part due to Knowles's authenticity in describing the experience of coming of age in wartime. While the book is not strictly autobiographical, Knowles considered it emotionally autobiographical. Although he would continue to write throughout his life, none of his subsequent books received critical acclaim.

There are no battle scenes in *A Separate Peace*, but war is omnipresent in the novel. Some critics have even argued that war is a character in the book. Because he lived through the experience, Knowles captured, as no writer has before or since, the experience of a teenage boy in a prep school during wartime: although he lives in a sheltered, academic environment, he feels the effects of a distant war and anticipates his own involvement in it.

Of the many effects World War II had on education, perhaps the most visible was the age of the teachers and their distance from students. As Knowles wrote in the *Exonian* (the school's newspaper) of his experiences at Exeter:

> All the faculty here were between fifty and seventy years old when I first entered Exeter in the fall of 1942. I had a young French teacher and one other young teacher but they had left for the war by midyear. All of the faculty on the campus were so much older than we were, that we had no connection with them. They just were too old, too tired, and too busy. One of the reasons that Gene and Finny develop this

intensely close friendship is that they had no one to relate to; no older person to pattern themselves on, to look and talk things over with, they only had each other. All the students really had to relate to each other.

Although Exeter attempted to maintain a normal environment for students during World War II, the age of the teachers and other conditions imposed by wartime meant a very different academic environment for students in the 1942–1945 era. Since many faculty members were serving in the armed forces, their positions were filled by substitutes, many of whom had little knowledge of the school's traditions and most of whom were beyond draft age. Given the scarcity of teachers, classes were larger. All of these factors contributed to a lack of connection between faculty and students.

Additionally, a program termed the Anticipatory Program was developed at Exeter to ensure that students would graduate before getting drafted. This program had two purposes—to accelerate graduation by taking advantage of summer semesters and to introduce into the curriculum courses that would better prepare students to succeed in military service. The army and navy officers' training programs were finding that officer candidates were woefully deficient in science and math. In fact, the Naval Officers' Training Corps found that 62 percent of its candidates failed an arithmetic reasoning test.

Knowles was a participant in the Anticipatory Program, attending summer sessions in 1943 and 1944. In 1944, he took two mathematics and one French course. By virtue of the Anticipatory Program, Knowles completed his sophomore through senior years in two years. It is the events of his first summer session, the summer of 1943, that Knowles writes about in *A Separate Peace*.

The novel reflects other changes that wartime imposed on daily life at the school, among them the cessation of maid service for students and the necessity of participating in extracurricular activities such as community service. Finny deplores the lack of maid service in the novel, and there are descriptions of the students at Devon School picking apples at a local orchard and helping to clear snow from railroad tracks as part of their wartime efforts. Even sports take on the effects of war, as the Devon students invent a game called blitzball, a wordplay on *blitzkrieg*, a German word meaning "lightning attack."

Despite the efforts of Exeter and other educational institutions to maintain normalcy for students, wartime is not a time of normalcy, and the presence of a distant war being fought is foreshadowed by many daily occurrences. In his accurate depiction of how a distant war affects the lives of students at a prep school, Knowles created a war novel that takes place far from the battlefields, but that brilliantly succeeds in its mission: to identify the causes of war in the human heart.

The articles that follow explore the meaning of war in *A Separate Peace* and also examine coming of age for young men in wartime, including in wartime today.

Chronology

1926
John Knowles is born in the coal-mining town of Fairmont, West Virginia, on September 16, the third of four children of James Myron and Mary Beatrice Shea Knowles. His father is a vice president of Consolidated Coal Company.

1932–1941
Knowles attends public schools in Fairmont.

1942
Knowles transfers to Phillips Exeter Academy, a prestigious prep school in New Hampshire, in his sophomore year.

1943
Knowles attends a summer wartime session at Phillips Exeter called the Anticipatory Program. He becomes a member of a group known as the Suicide Society—so named because the members make risky leaps from a tree into a nearby river.

1944–1946
Knowles graduates from Phillips Exeter in August and enters Yale University in the fall. After a short time, he enlists in the U.S. Army Air Force, where he is assigned to the aviation cadet program. He spends eight months in the cadet training program and qualifies as a pilot before being discharged from the service in 1945 following the ending of World War II. He returns to Yale in 1946.

1947
Knowles begins submitting short stories to the *Yale Record*, the college humor magazine.

1948
Knowles begins working for the *Yale Daily*, the campus newspaper, and is elected to its editorial staff.

1949

Knowles writes a novel that he presents to the faculty as his senior essay and graduates from Yale with a bachelor's degree in English.

1950–1952

Knowles works as a reporter and drama critic for the *Hartford Courant* in Connecticut.

1952–1956

Knowles travels to England, Italy, and France and meets Thornton Wilder, who becomes his writing mentor. Knowles writes a novel titled *Descent to Proselito* that is accepted for publication, but acting on the advice of Wilder, he withdraws the novel from publication. On returning from his travels, Knowles settles in New York and becomes a freelance journalist, contributing to *Holiday* magazine. In 1953 his first short story, "A Turn in the Sun," is published in *Story Magazine*.

1956

Cosmopolitan magazine publishes the short story "Phineas," which contains the basic theme for *A Separate Peace*.

1956–1960

Knowles joins the editorial staff of *Holiday* and moves to Philadelphia. He begins work on *A Separate Peace*.

1959

After being rejected by eleven U.S. publishers, *A Separate Peace* is published by Secker & Warburg in London and receives positive reviews from the UK press.

1960

Based on the favorable UK reception, Macmillan accepts *A Separate Peace* for publication and publishes it in February. The novel receives critical acclaim and wins the Rosenthal

Award from the National Institute of Arts and Letters and the William Faulkner Award for the most promising first novel of a new author. Knowles resigns from *Holiday* to become a full-time fiction writer and to travel. He sets out on a two-year tour of Europe and the Middle East.

1962

Knowles publishes *Morning in Antibes,* which was based on his visit to the French Riviera. The book earns mostly negative reviews.

1963–1964

Knowles serves as writer in residence at the University of North Carolina at Chapel Hill.

1964

Knowles publishes a collection of essays about his travels in the Middle East titled *Double Vision: American Thoughts Abroad.*

1966

Knowles's third novel, *Indian Summer,* is dedicated to Thornton Wilder.

1968–1969

Knowles serves as writer in residence at Princeton University and publishes a short story collection, *Phineas: Six Stories.*

1970

Knowles takes up year-round residence in a writers' community in Southampton, New York. His neighbors include Truman Capote, Willie Morris, and Irwin Shaw.

1971

The Paragon, Knowles's fourth novel, is published.

1972

The film version of *A Separate Peace* is released.

1974
Spreading Fires, Knowles's fifth novel, is published.

1978
A Vein of Riches, a novel about the coal-mining business in West Virginia, is published.

1981
A sequel to *A Separate Peace* titled *Peace Breaks Out* is published.

1983
A Stolen Past, a companion piece to *The Paragon*, is published.

1986
The Private Life of Axie Reed is published. Knowles starts an appointment as a creative writing teacher at Florida Atlantic University.

1993
A memoir, *Backcasts: Memories and Recollections of Seventy Years as a Sportsman*, is published.

2001
Knowles dies on November 29 in Fort Lauderdale, Florida.

Social Issues in Literature

CHAPTER 1

Background on John Knowles

The Life of John Knowles

Robert M. Nelson and Hallman Bell Bryant

Robert M. Nelson is professor of English emeritus at the University of Richmond. Hallman Bell Bryant is a professor of English at Clemson University and the author of A Separate Peace: The War Within.

Although Knowles wrote nine novels, only his first, A Separate Peace, *is considered a critical success, state Nelson and Bryant in the following essay. Inspired by the author's preparatory school days at Phillips Exeter Academy,* A Separate Peace *is concerned with the duality present in the New England character, a character that contains both stern Protestantism and a wild streak. To convey dualism, Knowles frequently creates alter egos in his fiction. In* A Separate Peace, *the characters of Gene Forrester and Phineas represent the two warring aspects of the New England character, the authors contend.*

John Knowles, the third of four children of James Myron and Mary Beatrice Shea Knowles, was born in Fairmont, West Virginia. He has an older brother and sister who are twins, and a younger sister. Knowles left West Virginia at fifteen to attend the Phillips Exeter Academy in New Hampshire during the World War II years. After graduating in 1945 he enlisted in the U.S. Army Air Force Aviation Cadet Program, eventually qualifying as pilot. Following his discharge after eight months, Knowles attended Yale University, serving briefly as an assistant editor for the *Yale Alumni* magazine after graduating in 1949; he then worked from 1950 to 1952 as a reporter and occasional drama critic for the *Hartford Courant*. Knowles was a freelance writer from 1952 to 1956. After a year or so abroad, touring Italy and southern France and writing his first novel, "Descent into Proselito" (which he decided not to publish, partly on the advice of his mentor Thornton Wilder), Knowles returned to the United States in 1955. He took up residence in the Hell's Kitchen section of New York City, where he shared an apartment with actor Bradford Dillman. He wrote occasional drama reviews while his first short stories (including "A Turn with the Sun" in 1953 and "Phineas" in 1956) were being published. During this period he continued to benefit from Wilder's interest in his work and began to write *A Separate Peace*.

A Separate Peace Was a Major Success

After *Holiday* magazine published his article on Phillips Exeter Academy in late 1956, Knowles moved to Philadelphia in 1957 to assume the post of associate editor for *Holiday*. During this time *A Separate Peace* was published, first in England (1959) and then in the United States (1960). When it became clear soon after its American publication that *A Separate Peace* was to be highly successful, Knowles, then thirty-four, resigned his editorship in August 1960 to embark on a two-year tour of Europe and the Middle East. His 1964 travelogue, *Double Vision: American Thoughts Abroad*, recounts his sojourn. His second novel, *Morning in Antibes* (1962), was published while Knowles was still abroad. Established as a professional writer, Knowles returned from Europe and moved to New York City, where he lived throughout the 1960s while continuing to travel abroad for short periods. During these years he served as a writer-in-residence, first at the University of North Carolina for the 1963–1964 session and then at Princeton in 1968–1969. His third novel, *Indian Summer*, which was dedicated to Thornton Wilder, was published in 1966, and a collection of short stories, *Phineas*, appeared in 1968. Two of his essays were published in the *New York Times*: "Where Does a Young Writer Find His Real Friends?" in 1962 and "The Writer-in-

Residence" in 1965. In 1970, the year his father died, Knowles took up permanent residence in Southampton, Long Island, where his neighbors in nearby villages have included Truman Capote, Winston Groom, Willie Morris, and Irwin Shaw. His fourth novel, *The Paragon*, appeared in 1971, followed by *Spreading Fires* in 1974 and *A Vein of Riches* in 1978. A motion picture version of *A Separate Peace* was released in 1972. *Peace Breaks Out*, designed to be a "companion piece" to *A Separate Peace*, was published in 1981, followed by *A Stolen Past* (which can be read as a companion piece to *The Paragon*) in 1983. His most recent novel is *The Private Live of Axie Reed*, published in 1986. Outside of commentaries on *A Separate Peace*, there has been little serious critical attention paid to Knowles's work.

Knowles Work Is Distinguished by Its Sense of Place

The settings of Knowles's novels reflect those environments he feels most influenced him. *A Vein of Riches*, which traces the fortunes of the Catherwood family from 1909 until 1924, is set in Middleburg, West Virginia, a coal-boom community not unlike Fairmont. The Phillips Exeter Academy takes on fictional form as the Devon school, where Gene Forrester spends most of the World War II years in *A Separate Peace*; the academy appears again (though less recognizably) as the Wetherford Country Day School attended by both Cleet Kinsolving and Neil Reardon prior to World War II in *Indian Summer*. Cleet returns to Connecticut after his military discharge in 1945 to see his brother off to Yale; in *The Paragon*, Louis Colfax comes to Yale in 1953 following an early discharge from the U.S. Marine Corps; and in *A Stolen Past* the narrator returns to Yale, his alma mater, to deliver an address and to review the life he created there thirty years previously. Knowles's own strong affinity during the early 1950s and early 1960s for the French Riviera is reflected in the settings of both *Morning*

Author John Knowles, who explored the concept of war in his novel A Separate Peace. *AP Images.*

in Antibes and *Spreading Fires* (which takes place at the villa Mas Tranquilitat, "overlooking Cannes").

Knowles's talent for describing local atmosphere, nurtured during his years with *Holiday*, has been frequently admired by his critics and is one of the mainstays of his appeal as a fiction writer. Knowles typically employs local description to forward the thesis that cultures are to a significant degree products of their geographical limitations, so that individual personalities are to be understood as ultimately shaped as much by the characteristics of their native climates and terrains as by heredity. The wanderlust of many of Knowles's protagonists reflects their needs to escape the subtle determinism of such environmental shaping. This thesis plays an especially strong part in the thematic development of his two Mediterranean novels as well as in *Indian Summer,* in which Cleet Kinsolving's desire to "roll out his life full force" is complemented by his "fear of being trapped" into returning to Wetherford, Connecticut, his small hometown. In *The Paragon* the "irascible climate" of Connecticut shapes a people who become "unresting, ever on the alert to what's next, brittle from the fatigue of ever adapting to their commanding climate." A similar line of speculation about how climate and geography determine the characteristic "climates" of various national cultures runs throughout *Double Vision: American Thoughts Abroad,* a collection of impressions gathered during Knowles's transatlantic junkets to England, southern France, Greece, and the Middle East. In *Double Vision,* Knowles tests his own acquired assumptions and expectations against a variety of external milieus; this process of self-testing is a major recurring motif in his novels, and Knowles's work is perhaps best understood as his series of attempts to work out the psychological implications of his crucial observation in *Double Vision* that "The American character is unintegrated, unresolved, a careful Protestant with a savage stirring in his insides, a germ of native American wildness thickening in his throat."

The Duality of Character

The idea for Knowles's first published novel, *A Separate Peace,* grew out of his short story "Phineas," which appeared in *Cosmopolitan* in May 1956. Frequently compared critically to J. D.

Salinger's *The Catcher in the Rye* (1951) and written despite Wilder's initial skepticism about the feasibility of the project, *A Separate Peace* is today one of the most widely read postwar American novels; it was in its sixty-fourth Bantam paperback run in March 1986, with a total of more than seven million copies in print. It won in 1960 the first William Faulkner Foundation Award for a notable first novel as well as the 1960 Rosenthal Award of the National Institute of Arts and Letters.

A Separate Peace represents Knowles's discovery of those psychological forces informing what he came to call in 1964 the prototypically New England "American character." This paradigmatic self is composed of two elements: the "germ of wildness," an essentially libidinal, creative primary element bent on expressing itself upon the world, and the "cautious Protestant," a secondary element committed essentially to defending, protecting, and conserving that primary self. The impulses and urges of the primary self manifest themselves in the form of anarchic human needs and desires and in the emotions of love and hate; the most obvious manifestations of the secondary self in Knowles's work are the institutions— governments, academic curricula, cultural ethos—which evolve out of the impulse of the secondary self but which, once created, take on an independently self-protective character and end up stifling the very spirit they exist ontologically [dealing with the nature of being] to protect. At their deepest level Knowles's novels are designed to isolate and study these two complementary but conflicting elements in the American character; hence the frequent appearance of doubles and alter-ego figures in his work. The novels focus upon the limited variety of adaptive strategies his protagonists invent to reconcile the urges within themselves to the prevailing shaping forces—the characteristic "givens" of culture and climate in which Knowles sets them.

The retrospective first-person point of view of *A Separate Peace* allows Gene Forrester to review the disintegration of his adolescent personality and the subsequent process of reintegration through the detaching distance of fifteen years, a distance which enables Knowles's protagonist to analyze as well as evaluate the evolution of his identity. As a prototype of the American character, Gene comes to Devon school controlled by the "cautious Protestant" in his character; various cultural and climatic images of conservatism at the school, including the adamantine First Academy Building, the frozen New Hampshire winterscape, and the "dull, dark green called olive drab" which he identifies as "the prevailing color of life in America" during the World War II years, all serve to reinforce this strain of his character. He is drawn to Brinker Hadley, the epitome of the "cautious Protestant." Student leader and class politician, Brinker is New England conservatism personified. At the same time, the repressed "germ of wildness" in Gene's character is attracted to Phineas, an indifferent student but a natural athlete and eccentric individualist who rules the playing fields of Devon during the summer session with a spirit of spontaneous anarchy. In contrast to the patriotic (and military) olive drab, which is the color of defensive conservatism for Gene, Phineas's emblem is an outrageously bright pink shirt.

The Development of Adolescent Personality

Gene's shifts of allegiance between these two projected versions of his own potential identity constitute "a study," according to Knowles, "of how adolescent personality develops, identifying with an admired person, then repudiating that person." Gene's early attempts to identify with Phineas (by reluctantly joining the Super Suicide Society, by accompanying Phineas on an overnight trip to the Atlantic Ocean) activate a conflict between the "cautious Protestant" and the "germ of wildness" within Gene's character, a conflict won by the cautious Protestant. When Gene causes Phineas to break a leg in a fall from the jumping tree, from which boys have been jumping into the river as a test of courage, Gene is forced to recognize the part of himself which identifies with Phineas. After Phineas has left school to recuperate from his injury, Gene secretly tries on Phineas's pink shirt and finds it fits. Gene's attempts to cultivate this awakened "germ of wildness" within himself are inhibited, however, by the presence of Brinker Hadley, who moves into the room across the hall from Gene's and immediately forces Gene to confront his disloyalty. Guided by Brinker, Gene decides to enlist in the armed forces, thus reducing the pains of coming to terms with his evolving identity by letting the military design his identity for him. Before Gene actually enlists, Phineas reappears at school, and Gene once again finds himself unable to repudiate completely either the anarchic forces within himself or his conservative defenses against those forces. Tutored by Phineas, Gene begins to train himself for the chimerical 1944 Olympics.

At the same time, Brinker, having lost his direct sway over Gene's allegiances, "had begun a long, decisive sequence of withdrawals from school activity ever since the morning I deserted his enlistment plan"; having changed his uniform from "well-bred clothes" to "khaki pants supported by a garrison belt," Brinker represents Gene's own lessening but nonetheless active commitment to the prevailing olive-drab way of life. As attractive as Phineas's "choreography of peace" is to Gene, the part of himself which identifies with Phineas's emotional hedonism once again finds itself at odds with the relentless shaping forces of the outside world, which finally intrude upon Devon irresistibly in the term of a telegram from Elwin "Leper" Lepellier, a schoolmate who enlisted and has gone "psycho" in boot camp.

Gene sees in Leper's condition a warning against going out into the world unprepared for dealing with hostility, a reminder that the "cautious Protestant" is a necessary element of an identity which hopes to survive in the world. Thus reminded of his dual commitment, but once again unable to reconcile the unintegrated forces within and without himself, Gene becomes a helpless observer of a climactic kangaroo court scene in which Phineas, and by extension the part of Gene identifying with Phineas, is put on trial by Brinker for refusing to cooperate with the "givens" of a world at war, with Leper serving as chief witness for the prosecution. Phineas rejects the trial, only to stumble blindly down the marble stairs of the First Academy Building, incurring a second and ultimately fatal fracture of his leg. Gene then isolates himself, at least temporarily, from these three characters and by extension their three separate strategies for coming to terms with one's self in the world; thus removed from the shaping forces of his past, he finally succeeds in achieving an integrated "double vision" which fuses, albeit tenuously, the warring parts of his character. The "separate peace" of the title refers to this valuable but temporary act of self-integration, which produces a personality that is a replication of neither of the essential forces which generated it but rather a delicate orchestration of those forces. . . .

Knowles Is a Master Craftsman

Knowles's reputation is based almost entirely on his achievement in *A Separate Peace*. Only occasionally has any of his subsequent works received unqualified praise in a major book review, and none has drawn the substantial critical attention usually paid to a writer of Knowles's stature. At its best, Knowles's work is generally regarded as showing admirably his "understanding of emotion and a sensitivity to the psychological struggles between love and enmity, between loyalty and freedom, between the need to accept guilt and the need to be absolved from it"; the flaws in his later work are generally attributed to a characteristic "mechanical neatness" in Knowles's handling of plot and setting as vehicles for dramatizing these psychological struggles, a handling which strikes many reviewers as being contrived. Critics both pro and con, however, generally concur in their assessment of Knowles as both a master craftsman and a serious student of that seemingly irreducible dualism he perceives at the heart of the American character.

Knowles Credits Phillips Exeter Academy for His Success

John Knowles

John Knowles was an American novelist. He is best known for his first novel, A Separate Peace, *which won the William Faulkner Foundation Prize and was later made into a film.*

In the following viewpoint, Knowles expresses his gratitude for the important and formative role his education at Phillips Exeter Academy had on his life. In contrast to many of his classmates, who had New England backgrounds, Knowles grew up in the coal mining hills of West Virginia. The academic discipline he learned at Exeter, Knowles claims, prepared him for Yale University and enabled him to write A Separate Peace. *During his time at Exeter, the atmosphere changed considerably because of World War II, and Knowles speculates that the sobering background of war may have helped make the students more resilient.*

Exeter was, I suspect, more crucial in my life than in the lives of most members of my class, and conceivably, than in the lives of almost anyone else who ever attended the school. It picked me up out of the hills of West Virginia, forced me to learn to study, tossed me into Yale (where I was virtually a sophomore by the time I entered), and a few years later inspired me to write a book, my novel *A Separate Peace*, which, eschewing false modesty, made me quite famous and financially secure.

John Knowles, "A Special Time, a Special School," *Exeter Bulletin*, Summer 1995, pp. 1–4. Copyright © 2008 the Trustees of Phillips Exeter Academy, Exeter, New Hampshire 03833-2460. Reproduced by permission.

Falling in Love with Exeter

My father was in the coal business in West Virginia. Both dad and mother were, however, originally from Massachusetts; New England, to them, meant the place to go if you really wanted an education. My brother had, to be sure, gone to Mercersburg Academy in Pennsylvania, but then he dutifully went off to Dartmouth, deep in deepest New Hampshire.

I was expected to follow him to Mercersburg, but picking up a catalog one day which was lying around the house, the catalog of Phillips Exeter Academy, I found a preliminary application form on the last page and, just for the hell of it, filled it out and mailed it.

Soon, entrance examinations were arranged for me at the local high school, administered by the principal no less. Exeter was clearly an important place. I knew little else about it, knew no one who had ever gone there, and, although my family visited New England most summers, I had never seen the school.

I possessed a certain amount of calculating cleverness at that time, and when the English entrance examination called for an essay on a novel of my choice, I knew better than to pick some commercial work like [Margaret Mitchell's] *Gone with the Wind*, opting instead for a novel I knew to be a classic, [Charlotte Brontë's] *Jane Eyre*.

That essay must have been pretty good because the other tests revealed that I knew little Latin after two years of it in the local school, and that I was almost entirely bereft of math.

I was put back one year and admitted as a lower-middler in September 1942.

It quickly seemed probable that I would flunk out. In the first marking period, I got a grade of 28 in mathematics, 14 in physics. Then somehow or other I knuckled down, learned by myself how to study, discovered I had a brain which had more potential than a knack for writing, and by the end of that first

31

term, I was passing every course comfortably. The school gave me a $100 grant as some kind of prize.

Meanwhile, I was falling in love with Exeter. I wasn't sure I liked the guys much—there was Stan Pleninger [class of] '45, in Sleeper House with me, who became a pal, but so many of the others seemed at first to be too Eastern for me, too Yankee, too tough. They largely left me alone, and I them. Mel Dickenson '45 and I eventually established something of a friendship: we used to have intense leg-wrestling matches under the table in Mr. Whitman's American history class—he won. Ted Lamont '44 became a friend, as did some of the boys on the swimming team, like our diver Joe Palmer.

As a kid from a border state, I found the New Hampshire winter breathtakingly cold—for a while I didn't think I could breathe there at all—but I survived to return for the summer session of 1943 in order to catch up the year I had been put back.

It was that summer that I realized I had fallen in love with Exeter. Most students don't experience summer there: I did so for two consecutive summers, 1943 and 1944. In other words, I was almost continuously at Exeter from September 1942 through August 1944, when I graduated. We're talking total Exeter immersion here.

The great trees, the thick clinging ivy, the expanses of playing fields, the winding black-water river, the pure air all began to sort of intoxicate me. Classroom windows were open; the aroma of flowers and shrubbery floated in. We were in shirt sleeves; the masters were relaxed. Studies now were easy for me. The summer of 1943 at Exeter was as happy a time as I ever had in my life.

Everything fit. There was a lively, congenial group of students in Peabody Hall that summer, many of them from other schools, accelerating like me. One was David Hackett from Milton Academy, on whom I later modeled Phineas in *A Separate Peace*. A great friend of Bobby Kennedy's, he later served under Bobby in the Justice Department. We really did have a club whose members jumped from the branch of a very high tree into the river as initiation. The only elements in *A Separate Peace* which were not in that summer were anger, envy, violence, and hatred. There was only friendship, athleticism, and loyalty.

War Changed the Exeter Experience

Returning to Exeter for the fall term of 1943, I found that a charged, driven time had come to the school. I remember how virtually all the younger masters disappeared one by one, and old men became our only teachers. Too old to be in any way companions to us, they forced the class of 1943 to be reliant very much on itself, isolated. Maybe that made us stronger in a certain way. There was apple-harvesting "for the war," railroad-yard clearance "for the war," numerous collection drives "for the war," and all those patriotic movies in the gym with Spencer Tracy, or Van Johnson, of someone heroically bombing Tokyo. The massively crowded trains, hopelessly behind schedule, we had to take to try to get home for holidays. Nobody had gasoline except people like my father, in a basic industry with special allowances. All those maps of heretofore strange parts of the world with strange names like Anzio and Guadalcanal and Saipan [battlefields of World War II].

Looking back, I think we were all quite mature, surprisingly responsible. In earlier wars, boys of our age had just gone off to raise hell or enlist or both, but we stayed dutifully at our desks doing tomorrow's homework. Tomorrow, they felt in 1862 or 1917, you died perchance, so discipline went by the board, and they cut loose. We didn't; I don't know why not. Was it that our war was so overwhelmingly vast, the first truly world war, that it overawed us into being dutiful, responsible, approaching it one step at a time?

I know that I studied diligently. I took both Latin I and Latin II with Mr. Galbraith. A finer, more inspiring teacher I never encountered. By the time he was through with me, I thoroughly understood the nature and structure of a language, and he had crucially influenced both my thinking and the way I expressed it in words. I am the writer I am because of him.

In fact, despite the giant holes in the faculty caused by the war, the best teaching I ever experienced was at Exeter. Yale was a distinct let-down afterward. The teachers there either read their year-in-year-out lectures to us in large auditoriums, or, meeting us in small groups, seemed preoccupied with their extramural careers or reputations or whatever. They did not seem to be there primarily for us. It was Exeter which taught me how to approach new material, organize it, and express it.

Exeter, in those emergency years, also managed to keep a full athletic program going, and I know very many of us are grateful for that. I arrived at Exeter quite sure that I was a good swimmer, and it came as quite a shock when my buddy down the hall, Pleninger, beat me in the first time try-outs with Dan Fowler '45, and proceeded to be faster than I was ever after, and deservedly became the captain of the varsity team.

Swimming isn't the most thrilling sport in the world, far from it; it's a damn bore most of the time, but it does make you healthy and gives you a good body. I finished first as the anchor man in the final, decisive relay against Andover, to become an athletic mini-hero for about 15 minutes.

You can see by now how I admire the school and love it. When the film version of *A Separate Peace* was made, Exeter cooperated and allowed Paramount to shoot all over the campus and inside the buildings.

The novel has one peculiarity for a school novel: It never attacks the place; it isn't an exposé; it doesn't show sadistic masters or depraved students, or use any of the other school-novel sensationalistic clichés. That's because I didn't experience things like that there. I found there a gorgeous world prepared to shape me up, and I tried to present and dramatize that.

A *Separate Peace* Contains Many Autobiographical Aspects

John Knowles

John Knowles was an American novelist. He is best known for his first novel, A Separate Peace, *which won the William Faulkner Foundation Prize and was later made into a film.*

In the following article, Knowles describes his intentions in writing A Separate Peace, *a book that he calls autobiographical for the way it expresses the emotional truth of his summer semester at Phillips Exeter Academy in 1943. This semester occurred against the backdrop of World War II, and the war preoccupied the thoughts of the students, Knowles states. He explains that he wrote* A Separate Peace *to explore the conflicts the war raised in him—pacifism and aggression, loyalty and rivalry, love and hate, and fear and idealism.*

What I set out to do in [*A Separate Peace*] was to unscramble, plumb, and explain what had happened during a very peculiar summer at Phillips Exeter Academy in New Hampshire, where I was a sixteen-year-old summer-session student in 1943. It was just as World War II was turning in our favor, and were we boys going to be in it or not? And what was war, and what was aggression, and what were loyalty and rivalry, what were goodness and hate and fear and idealism, all of them swirling around us during that peculiar summer?

Gene Forrester Is Based on Knowles

I wrote the book to dramatize and work through those questions.

The story itself was certainly not the usual kind of material for a best seller. The narrator, Gene Forrester, bright and athletic, and his roommate, the extraordinary schoolboy athlete Phineas, are taking an accelerated course through the Devon School in New Hampshire so as to get into World War II before it ends. Beneath their great friendship in these idyllic countrified surroundings there is a lurking rivalry, hostility, and destructiveness. During a dangerous game of jumping from a high tree into the river, Phineas is gravely injured.

Gene is suspected of having provoked this "accident" out of buried resentment, and sometimes he thinks so himself. One of their group meanwhile goes off to the military service and soon after creeps back to Devon, "psycho." And then the students stage a mock trial to try Gene, and the book moves on to its climax. It is a schoolboy story and it is also an allegory about the sources of war.

I based the narrator, Gene Forrester, on myself; Phineas on my friend, the exceptional student athlete David Hackett. We were in school together for only one summer, at Exeter Academy; his athletic career was conducted at Milton Academy outside Boston and at McGill University in Montreal. There he excelled in many sports, preeminently in hockey, qualifying for the U.S. Olympic Ice Hockey Team in 1948.

Dave was not crippled by a fall from a tree in 1943, but I reversed matters while writing A Separate Peace and turned a real, not very serious accident to me into a fateful fictional one for him. This reversal made it possible to show the darker streaks of human nature. If I were going to make my point, then the Phineas character would have to be the victim.

David went on to work for his lifelong friend Robert Kennedy in the Justice Department in Washington, to marry happily and have five children, and to view with some bemusement the short, legendary, and tragic life of Phineas, a character he inspired and very much resembled, up to a point.

Some of the other characters in the novel were loosely based on other students: Brinker Hadley on Gore Vidal, for instance. People react in a singular way when they find you have constructed a fictional character with them in mind. Gore feels that the muses intended *A Separate Peace* for his pen and that only some inexplicable blunder on Mount Helicon [home of the gods in Greek mythology] caused it to descend upon me.

A Separate Peace Differs from *The Catcher in the Rye*

A British reviewer remarked that one would think, on reading *A Separate Peace*, that the author "had never heard of J.D. Salinger." His novel about a preparatory schoolboy had been published several years before I sat down to write mine and had been very widely read and discussed and admired. When I was about a third of the way into my book I ran across a copy of *The Catcher in the Rye*. Always having meant to read it, I started in. Oh my God, I said to myself on about page 10, a teenage boy! In a prep school! This thing could *influence* me, if I let it. I closed the book and only returned to it when mine was in galleys. Then I read and admired it very much. They are very different books. His is a 360-degree circumambulating of one fascinating character. Mine is linear, a narrative involving two and then four interrelating characters.

Isn't such a success with your first book, people ask, a kind of curse, since everything that follows will be compared unfavorably to it? No, because, first of all, it freed me from having to teach school or be a journalist, enabling me to devote myself entirely to fiction writing. And it gave me a public identity.

The one limiting result of this success is that my later work was expected to resemble *A Separate Peace*. My readers wanted my books to be set in schools. They loved *Peace Breaks*

A cover to John Knowles's novel A Stolen Past *(1983), which, like* A Separate Peace, *takes place in a school setting.* Copyright © Henry Holt and Company.

Out, which is a "companion novel" to *A Separate Peace*. They also approved of *The Paragon* and of my most recent novel, *A Stolen Past*, about a Russian princess and her son, set mostly at Yale. Other books, if they were not set in schools, got a cooler reception. They weren't really Knowles novels.

A Separate Peace Is Emotionally Autobiographical

A different kind of unsettling experience occurred when the novel was made into a movie. Paramount released *A Separate Peace* in 1972, and I went to see it in fear and trepidation. But it was very different from what I anticipated. They had certainly not vulgarized the work; in fact, the movie was almost painfully faithful to the book. It had been gorgeously photographed at Exeter Academy, and they had created and solved great difficulties by shooting there during each of the four seasons, shutting down production in the intervals. John Heyl and Parker Stevenson, neither of whom had dreamed of being an actor, turned in effective and genuine performances under the direction of Larry Peerce.

What was hard to bear were the emotions embodied by those young actors filmed in the very place where the original events transpired. Revealing emotion didn't bother me in words, in a book, but on that great big screen it all seemed too painful, too personal.

The book is autobiographical. By no means did all the incidents happen as portrayed, but the emotional truth of it comes out of my life. "You have to strip yourself naked," [F.] Scott Fitzgerald wrote. Thornton Wilder, discarding an early attempt at a novel by me, wrote in a letter: "Everything in this novel lacks intensity. . . . Find a subject which you are deeply moved about, very much absorbed in. . . . Select your next subject from the compelling elements in your life. . . . It is from our most vital subjectivity that we write. . . ." Well, *A Separate Peace* really should have been dedicated to Thornton.

All of this is essentially literary gossip, and what counts, in the long run, is what the book has meant to readers, so many millions of readers, and why.

A Separate Peace is one long and abject confession, a mea culpa [acknowledgment of fault], a tale of crime—if a crime had been committed—and of no punishment, or only interior punishment. It is a story of growth through tragedy. Young people, on their deepest emotional level, respond to that. It makes not the slightest difference that the story's externals may be totally foreign to them. In the novel there is not a girl in sight; that means nothing—women of all ages and every background treat it as central to their view of life. It takes place among some privileged kids in a first-class preparatory school: that doesn't mean anything either. One of the most moving letters I ever got was from the teenage participants in a drug treatment program in the Bedford-Stuyvesant section of Brooklyn. Another was from a group of paraplegic veterans of the Vietnam War. Co-eds in Finland, old ladies in Italy, a murderer on death row in Utah—all have communicated their depth of feeling about the book.

These responses, of course, are the greatest reward *A Separate Peace* can bring or ever will bring to me. The book has affected millions of lives, influenced them deeply, modified what they saw and felt in the world about them. The ultimate importance of *A Separate Peace* is that it has reached out to the readers who need it.

Knowles Is Frequently Compared with J.D. Salinger

Elaine Woo

Elaine Woo is a staff writer for the Los Angeles Times.

In the following essay, which Woo wrote as an obituary for John Knowles, she discusses the critical acclaim the author received for A Separate Peace, *praise that was to elude him regarding his subsequent works.* A Separate Peace *deals with the universal theme of the battle between innocence and evil and does so in evocative prose. Woo notes that Knowles was often compared with J.D. Salinger, as both authors' most acclaimed work dealt with teenage angst in a preparatory school setting.*

Novelist John Knowles, whose 1960 book *A Separate Peace* became a modern classic for its sensitive evocation of adolescent conflict, died Thursday [November 29, 2001,] after a short illness at a convalescent home near Fort Lauderdale, Fla. He was 75.

A Separate Peace Eclipsed His Other Novels

Knowles' first and best-known work was based on his experiences at Phillips Exeter Academy, a well-known New Hampshire boarding school. Although he wrote eight other novels, none received the acclaim he earned with his debut work, which received the William Faulkner Foundation Prize and inspired a 1973 movie.

He did not seem bitter about the shadow *A Separate Peace* cast over his other novels, which include *Indian Summer*

(1966) and *Peace Breaks Out* (1981). His avowedly autobiographical debut novel, he often acknowledged, made him famous and gave him financial security.

Decades after its original publication, *A Separate Peace* was selling half a million copies a year and remains a staple of high school and college reading lists.

"Isn't that incredible?" he said in 1986. "And what touches me most, what pleases me most, is that people who are far removed from the world of prep schools love it."

One of the characters, Brinker, was based on Gore Vidal, who was a few years ahead of Knowles at Exeter in the mid-1940s. The two writers eventually became good friends.

"I have no memory of him when we were in school together," Vidal said Thursday from his home in Italy. "The next thing I know is he has published *A Separate Peace*, in which I play a cameo part as sort of a snoop. . . . Then I got to know him, because I thought *A Separate Peace* was a marvelous book. It was beyond anything he ever did later and anyone else had done of that sort, with the possible exception of [J.D. Salinger's] *Catcher in the Rye*."

When Knowles made his literary debut, one reviewer eagerly asked: "Is he the successor to Salinger for whom we have been waiting for so long?"

The parallels to Salinger's masterpiece, published a decade earlier, in 1951, were hard to ignore. Both dealt with the angst of prep school boys, and both were highly praised first novels.

Knowles was born in Fairmont, W. Va., where his father was in the coal business. His parents expected him to follow his older brother to a prep school in Pennsylvania, but Knowles—"just for the hell of it"—applied to Exeter. He cannily chose [Charlotte Brontë's] *Jane Eyre* as the topic of his essay for the school's English entrance exam and later reflected that the essay must have been good because his math and Latin scores were abysmal.

John Knowles is most often compared to author J.D. Salinger (pictured). AP Images.

Encouraged to Write by Thornton Wilder

Entering Exeter in fall 1942, Knowles was an indifferent student at first, more concerned with getting by than getting ahead.

He graduated in 1945 and joined the war effort as part of the Army Air Force's Aviation Cadet Program. Several months later, he entered Yale University, earning a bachelor's degree in 1949.

In the 1950s, Knowles spent much of his time as a journalist, first as a freelancer in Europe and later as an associate editor of *Holiday* magazine.

He became friends with playwright Thornton Wilder, who encouraged him to write. Knowles began to work on *A Separate Peace*, quitting journalism after its successful publication.

He drew heavily on his Exeter years because they were, he once said, "more crucial in my life than in the lives of most members of my class, and conceivably, than in the lives of almost anyone else who ever attended the school. It picked me up out of the hills of West Virginia, forced me to learn to study, tossed me into Yale . . . and a few years later inspired me to write . . ."

His pivotal time there began in summer 1943, when he took classes to make up for poor first-year grades. The teachers, or masters, were more relaxed and students felt more carefree, hanging from trees and frolicking on playing fields. Knowles kept company with a lively group of boys from other schools who, like him, needed to make up courses over the summer. It was, he said, "as happy a time as I ever had in my life."

Knowles and his friends formed a club called the Super Suicide Society of the Summer Session, which initiated members by requiring them to jump from the branch of a tall tree into the river. The club became a central element of *Peace*, as did one of its members, who inspired the character of Phineas, one of the novels two protagonists.

"We really did have a club whose members jumped from the branch of a very high tree into the river as initiation," Knowles told the *Exeter Bulletin* several years ago. "The only elements in *A Separate Peace* which were not in that summer were anger, envy, violence and hatred. There was only friendship, athleticism, and loyalty."

Peace turns on the complex friendship of two boys, Gene and Phineas, or Phinny, both students at a private school called Devon. Gene is academically gifted, while Phinny's power is on the playing field. The story is told through the eyes of Gene, whose insecurities and resentment of his friend's popularity lead to a tragic incident in which Phinny is badly injured falling out of a tree. Gene is later accused of causing Phinny's fall, which ends his athletic career. Phinny later injures himself again and dies on the operating table.

The passage in which Phinny is first injured is "a rich part of the novel. It's exquisite," said Charles Terry, who taught *Peace* in his courses at Exeter for 30 years. His students always debated whether Gene deliberately caused Phinny's crippling fall, as they have in many other classrooms.

Knowles himself refused to answer the question, preferring the ambiguity. "Was it deliberate or not? It is one of the great ambiguous stories," Vidal said. "One of the reasons Jack was taken very seriously in Europe was this was pure [existentialist writer Jean-Paul] Sartre."

Manuscripts Given to Alma Mater

The novel's enduring appeal also stems from its layered richness. It is a tale of innocence and evil, and an exploration of opposing selves. Knowles returned to these themes in his later works, but critics by and large judged those efforts far less positively.

Peace, he said in a 1986 interview, was in many ways "an albatross. Everything is compared unfavorably to it afterward."

In 1978, he went back to Exeter for a week to address students and alumni and review his handwritten manuscripts of *Peace*, which he donated to his alma mater.

"He was feeling despondent over the fact that all his books after *Separate Peace* never achieved the same acclaim," said Exeter librarian Jacquelyn Thomas.

One day, Knowles took her and John Heyl, the former Exeter student who played Phineas in the movie, to the woods to find the tree that he and his friends jumped off many years before. Straying far past the river, they could not find it. On the way back, he exclaimed, "There's the tree!" How they could be so sure no one knew, but Knowles at last was satisfied.

Finding the tree, he said in a letter to Thomas later, was "a particularly moving moment." "The hold the school has on me," he said, "is inextinguishable."

A Separate Peace and War

A *Separate Peace* Is a Pacifist Novel

Simon Raven

Simon Raven was a novelist, essayist, screenwriter, and literary critic. He is best known for his ten-volume saga of English upper-class life, Alms for Oblivion.

A Separate Peace, written by the American John Knowles, was first published in England after being rejected by numerous U.S. publishers. British critics, including Raven, gave the novel very positive reviews. In the following article, Raven calls A Separate Peace *a pacifist novel. The theme of the book is a rejection of war, Raven contends, with Gene and Phineas making a courageous, if doomed, stand against the folly of war.*

[*A* Separate Peace], modest as it is in tone, is likely to leave you thinking. The misuse of science now makes it necessary to articulate a new and purely practical form of Pacifism, a Pacifism which, free of crankiness and owing nothing to religious sensitivity, depends entirely on simple common sense. From now on, people must say, war will mean not only a shortage of cakes and ale but the end of everything. It is this form of protest, of personal withdrawal from political folly which, among other things, makes such pleasant reading of John Knowles's *A Separate Peace*. It is the story of two friends at a smart American preparatory school (for 'preparatory' read 'public' in this country [the UK]) at the time when America first joined the Second World War. In the beginning the younger boys are more or less ignored while their elders are hurriedly prepared for the blood bath; but as time goes on the whole school is efficiently geared to the

Simon Raven, "No Time for War," *The Spectator*, vol. 202, May 1, 1959, p. 630. Copyright © 1959 by *The Spectator*. Reproduced by permission of *The Spectator*.

conditioning of cannon-fodder, and every aspect of work and play comes to be valued, by masters who are themselves too old to fight, only in so far as it is a preparation for the trial to come. . . . Gene, the intellectually inclined narrator, has a fit of insane resentment and causes his athletic friend, Phineas, to break his leg. Phineas, so badly crippled that he will be out of the war in any case, broods over the separate peace thus forced upon him and eventually decides that the war is entirely spurious, that the whole thing has been thought up by [Franklin Delano] Roosevelt, [Winston] Churchill and the authorities in general simply because they are old men jealous of youth and pleasure. Once upon a time, Phineas says, all these kill-joys

> '. . . got really desperate and arranged the Depression. That kept the people who were young in the Thirties in their places. But they couldn't use that trick forever, so for us in the Forties they've cooked up this war fake.'

> 'Who are *they*, anyway?'

> 'The fat old men who don't want us crowding them out of their jobs. . . .'

A Futile Attempt to Deny War

Phineas, of course, is in part rationalising his annoyance at being out of something; but the more sensitive Gene accepts what he says as an important truth. So privately and together they resist the war and all it implies until reality makes itself felt—sickeningly so—in its own good time. . . . In emphasising the wider theme of this book, I have done less than justice to other matters—the quietly told story of the boys' relationship and its crises, the sweat and hopeless melancholy which pervades the whole. But then the real importance of Mr. Knowles's novel does indeed lie in its account of the attempt, made by two powerless individuals, to dissociate themselves from *them* and the follies for which *they* are responsible. It is an attempt strictly in accord with the principles of the 'common-sense' pacifism I described above—but an attempt doomed to painful failure unless *everyone* makes it. How silly the Generals on both sides, how silly *they* would look then. But Mr. Knowles makes it plain enough (if we hadn't guessed already) that quiet common sense is a feeble match for reality and the Generals: *they* are sure of the last word.

Knowles Explores the Roots of War in *A Separate Peace*

Hallman Bell Bryant

Hallman Bell Bryant is a professor of English at Clemson University in South Carolina.

Bryant maintains in the following excerpt that the central theme of A Separate Peace *is the notion that war is caused by evil in the human heart. The peaceful setting of Devon School contrasts starkly with reminders of the distant war being waged. Knowles uses various literary techniques adroitly to convey his theme, including imagery that evokes war and violence. By the novel's end, the narrator, Gene, has vanquished his internal enemy, which is self-ignorance. With his newfound knowledge, Gene is able to accept his military duty.*

The tenth chapter is a pivotal point in [*A Separate Peace*]. Knowles pushes closer here to the central theme of the novel—the presence of a blind, insane, ignorant evil in the heart of man that creates fear and causes hatred and destruction. Leper, with the unerring insight often found in the insane, probes Gene's conscience with his accusations and makes a private judgment on him that Gene will eventually have to acknowledge publicly. Leper's experience has forced him to "admit things" to himself; he understands that the same brutal forces that cause wars and necessitate armies are also present under the veneer of Gene's "good guy" personality. Gene, however, cannot accept Leper's wisdom of woe and rejects the whole of his experience, although Leper's problem—establishing a person's true identity—is ironically the same kind of identity crisis that Gene faces.

Hence, the episode in Vermont heightens the novel thematically as well, preparing for the subsequent culmination of events in the last three chapters, in which the tragic climax of the novel will turn on the reappearance of Leper. . . .

Devon School Represents a Sanctuary

The next two chapters of the novel describe the trial scene and Finny's second fall—events that lead up to the novel's tragic climax and prepare for the denouement, or final unravelling, of the plot in Chapter 13. As we have seen in the previous scene, the security of Devon, with its comforting illusions of a world at peace, is the creation of Phineas, whose view of conflict is limited to athletics. Gene's first sight of Finny upon his return sharply contrasts with his last glimpse of Leper: he finds his friend in the middle of a snowball fight. The childish activity and boyish joy in life it expresses are a world away from the adult conflict that led to Leper's mental crippling. Although Finny too has been wounded by the evil inherent in life, he has not let his spirit be blighted. He is, as Gene knows, the organizing principle behind the snowball fight. Although it is an outlandish idea, he has succeeded in getting the top boys of the senior class to engage in the fray, which takes place on the most remote part of the campus on grounds called "The Fields Beyond." Knowles here, as he does frequently throughout the novel, brings in a description of the physical background and gives it a metaphysical dimension. In this case it is onto the landscape that Gene wistfully projects his most deeply felt desire for a sanctuary from the mounting tension of his inner conflict. Standing on the edge of the woods watching Finny, Gene thinks that the trees represent something "primevally American, reaching in unbroken forests far to the north, into the great northern wilderness" and he wonders "whether things weren't simpler and better at the northern terminus of these woods, a thousand miles due north into the wilderness, somewhere deep in the Arctic, where the peninsula of trees which began at Devon would end at last in an untouched grove of pine, austere and beautiful."

In a retrospective aside, the narrator confides to the reader that he now knows there is "no such grove," but at that point in his life he imagined that it might be "just over the visible horizon." After his confrontation with Leper's insanity and the reexposure to the ugly truth of big own guilt, Gene's mind is deeply disturbed, and his need to return to Phineas and Devon is a reaction to the disorder and irrationality experienced during his mission to help Leper—which, paradoxically, has helped Leper very little but has provided Gene with an additional perspective on himself and a glimpse into the "heart of darkness." Gene, like Marlowe in [Joseph] Conrad's great short novel about madness and depravity [*Heart of Darkness*], is almost overcome by the vision of evil that he has witnessed, and he wants to insulate himself from anything disturbing. Thus, he seeks the same, ordered, Greek-inspired world Finny inhabits, a world that follows Olympian ideas and gives the prize to those soundest in body and spirit. Hence, he also sees the Devon woods in terms of the Edenic innocence that Finny represents. Life to Gene has become a "tangled" business, and the more he experiences existence beyond the groves of academe, the more he would like to evade it.

The Means, Not the End, Is Important to Finny

Gene's observations of Finny make up the rest of this scene and deserve comment. For instance, this scene is the last one in the novel where the reader sees Finny in his natural sphere—the world of games. Earlier we were given a lengthy description of Finny playing blitzball, and now Knowles provides us with a second look at Finny in his personal world of athletic competition. The activity takes place as winter is about to give way to spring, but there is still enough snow on the ground to make snowballs. In another passage of fine descrip-

The German city of Dresden lies in ruins after being bombed by Allied forces in 1945. In A Separate Peace, the characters must reconcile their peaceful prep-school surroundings with the harsh reality of a world at war. © Corbis.

tive writing, Knowles creates one of the most unusual but evocative *reverdies* [French term for poems celebrating spring-time] in literature. It is not that first robin, the usual herald of spring in New England, but the smell of the boys' clothing that reminds Gene of spring. Knowles writes, "Everywhere there was the smell of vitality in clothes, the vital something in wool and flannel and corduroy which spring releases. I had forgotten that this existed, this smell which instead of the first robin, or the first bud or leaf, means to me that spring has come." Paradoxically, the odor from these sturdy winter garments not only gives Gene happiness, because with it is the promise of new vitality and energy as the land revives after winter, but it also creates in his mind an uncertainty about the future and the sort of clothing he might wear in future springs, when he must change from civilian clothes to [military] khaki.

This scene suggests the actual wartime combat awaiting many of the "combatants" in the mock fight, who are described as the "cream of the school, the lights and leaders of the senior class . . .". Now, however, their commanding general is Phineas, and, despite being crippled and in a cast, his movements and coordination are hardly impaired, only noticeable now because his earlier grace had been so perfect. The point on which Knowles wants the reader to focus here is the unique way Finny plays games. He keeps changing sides in the fight, going over to the side that needs help, "betraying" his side to "heighten the disorder" and to keep one group from defeat or victory because, as Gene realizes, "no one was going to win or lose;" the fight was a game in which the main thing to Finny was the action, not the outcome. In sports as in life for Finny, the important thing is not the end but the means, hence his dedication to activities like blitzball, swimming, and jumping from trees that are invented forms of play, outside of the sanctions of organized sports, and, above all, games where no score is kept. People like Finny who do not play by the usual rules are the one whom life breaks, as [Ernest] Hemingway wrote, and although Finny, perhaps thinking of another metaphor from *A Farewell to Arms*, would like to think that the bone is "supposed to be stronger when it grows together over a place where it's been broken once," his case will prove the exception to the rule.

Just as the previous chapter was filled with portent for Gene, Chapter 11 contains many events that foreshadow Finny's fate. Gene, for instance, is alarmed by Finny's disregard for his injured leg during the snowball fight and reminds him that Dr. Stanpole had warned him to be careful not to fall again. Perhaps more ominous than all is that here Finny comes to terms with a truth that he has previously denied, the existence of a world at war. The revelation of Leper's experiences punctures Finny's willing suspension of disbelief about the war: "he quietly brought to a close all his special inventions which had carried us through the winter. Now the facts were reestablished, and gone were all the fantasies, such as the Olympic Games for A.D. 1944, closed before they had ever been opened."

The Reality of War Becomes Clear

There are two other scenes here that touch on the theme of war and also reveal how the illusions held by Gene and Finny over the winter were only temporary stays from historical reality, a reality that both boys, if they were honest with themselves, have known all along. As the school year moves into its final phase with the approach of spring and graduation for the senior class, the campus is host to many military officers, who speak to the students about the merits of their services. To Gene the various military programs that are set up on college campuses, such as the navy's V-5 and V-12 programs and the army's Special Training Program, appear more and more attractive because they seem very safe, peaceful and "almost like just going normally on to college." So, rather than choosing a university, as would have been the case in peacetime, the Devon class of 1943 is faced with the decision of which branch of the military to choose. The normal crisis for prep school students in this year is not where they will attend college; rather, it is where they will go to be prepared for the final battles of the war. As Gene says, "There was no rush to get into the fighting; no one seemed to feel the need to get into the infantry . . . The thing to be was careful and self-preserving. It was going to be a long war."

The Boys Admit the War Is Real

Gene's appraisal of himself and his classmates at this point reveals a retrospective wisdom, arising from a mature reflection on the events of his life, as he approaches his eighteenth birthday. However, in this stoic acceptance of the inevitable, we find an indication of a more composed and adult attitude. Gene is ready to accept his military responsibility, but he does not have any patriotic fantasies about war now. In an astute observation on the difference between the two worlds, military and the academic, that have been forced into an awkward collaboration by circumstances, Knowles writes, "Devon was by tradition and choice the most civilian of schools, and there was a certain strained hospitality in the way both the faculty and students worked to get along with the leathery recruiting officers who kept appearing on the campus . . . we could feel a deep and sincere difference between us and them, a difference which everyone struggled with awkward fortitude to bridge. It was as though [the warring Greek cities of] Athens and Sparta were trying to establish not just a truce but an alliance—although we were not as civilized as Athens and they were not as brave as Sparta."

The military theme and classical allusions are carried over into another scene that centers on Gene and Finny and shows two important sides of Phineas's character: his love of music and his distrust of conventional wisdom. Remember that Finny was first shown in this chapter doing something he loved—playing games—and when he next appears he is seen singing "A Mighty Fortress Is Our God." The insertion of this hymn being sung by Finny serves an important but subtle function. It reminds us that the ultimate protection and sanctuary from evil are not manmade military machines but rather something within the human heart. It is the force of the spirit that will, as the hymn goes, "Of mortal ills prevailing". Paradoxically, Finny, who has such great physical rhythm, is tone deaf and can't carry a tune; nevertheless, he loves all music profoundly.

The war theme appears in this chapter in the scene where Gene helps Finny with a Latin translation. The homework passage deals with "a surprise attack" on the Romans by the Gauls who ambush Caesar's legions in a swamp. Although Finny doubts if Gene's rather free translation will satisfy the literal-minded Latin teacher, he voices even greater doubt about the authenticity of Caesar, Rome, and the Latin language. He sweeps aside the whole concept of the reality of the events of two thousand years in the past. As emphatically as Huckleberry Finn [in Mark Twain's *The Adventures of Huckleberry Finn*], who discounted the Old Testament story of Moses by saying he did not take any "stock" in dead folks, Finny cannot accept a dead language, a dead empire, or a dead tyrant as facts that bear on the reality of his own existence. Books and teachers are also cynically regarded by Finny as conspirators who perpetuate historical illusions to keep the youth enslaved to remote facts. In another moment of candor, such as the earlier declaration of his friendship to Gene on the beach, Finny confesses to his roommate that it is important for him to believe in something. He adds, "I've got to believe in you, at least. I know you better than anybody." Of course, this statement is dramatically very ironic, and again Gene is not capable of making an adequate or honest response. At this point, Finny's pretense that the war is a hoax has to be admitted, since he has no choice but to believe Gene's account of Leper's crackup. In addition, he too has seen the frightened Leper hiding in the bushes near the school chapel, and he says, "I knew there was a real war on," to which Gene replies, "Yes, I guess it's a real war all right, but I liked yours a lot better." The boys have now come to the end of what Knowles equates to a "binge" of the imagination; they feel half-guilty but mutually amused, as cohorts who lived through an intoxicating experience and must now resume more decorous deportment. In their last moment of comraderie before the revelation of Gene's secret, "the sun was doing antics among the million specks of dust hanging between us and casting a brilliant, unstable pool of light on the floor." Incidentally, this intimate scene recalls the situation of shared light used to symbolize the symbiotic relationship in Chapter 4, where Finny sits opposite Gene at the study table with the lamp casting "a round yellow pool between us." The light is indeed fading, and the momentary stay against the truth that Gene and Finny had maintained over the better part of the school term is about to end. The fragile stability of the situation is shattered by the arrival in their room of Brinker at 10:05, who announces that a court of inquiry has been convened to get to the bottom of what happened at the tree.

Betrayal in the Tree Mirrors War

The trial scene that follows is the final episode of this chapter and precipitates the tragic catastrophe of the novel. Of all of the plot events in the novel, this one has seemed most problematical to commentators, who raise objections to the night court situation as a means to move the story to a conclusion. . . .

It is, of course, now a [moot] question whether Knowles could have found a less contrived situation than the trial to bring about the revelation of the full truth of Gene's treachery to Finny. Yet, as the scene is written, it very effectively evokes a mood of gloom and impending doom. The windows have a "deadened look" about them; the walls appear opaque with blackened canvasses of deceased headmasters' portraits and a dead World War I hero, and the ten members of the senior class in black robes all create an ominous tone. At the beginning of the investigation both Gene and Finny express contempt for Brinker's court, but when Brinker brings up the matter of the accident and hints that it was not just a fall, Finny admits that he has had the same suspicion but never allowed himself to think about it, because he could accept the fact that Gene might have caused his injury. His confidence in

Gene is shaken for the first time when Gene, under the pressure of Brinker's investigation, lies and claims that he was standing at the trunk of the tree, when Finny knows that he was with him out on the limb. The questioning turns to where Gene was, as Brinker refuses to believe that Gene cannot recall exactly where he was, and Finny, in a flash of recollection, cuts through to the truth, recalling that they climbed up the tree together to undertake a double jump. The members of the tribunal are not satisfied and demand a witness who can testify to the facts. Then Finny remembers that the AWOL [absent without leave (from military duty)] Leper has returned to Devon and can clear up the matter, because he was also at the tree. Finny has suggested Leper as a witness no doubt because he hopes that he can clear Gene. Gene, on the other hand, hopes only that Leper will appear so deranged that no one will believe him, thus legally making him an unreliable witness. Much to Gene's chagrin, Leper looks quite well and his manner is composed and lucid.

Leper's testimony lays bare in vividly imagistic terms what actually took place at the tree. He tells the boys assembled that although the sun was in his eyes, he saw both Gene and Finny standing on the limb in a blaze of light from the setting sun, whose rays were "shooting past them like—like golden machine-gun fire" and that their silhouettes looked "black as death standing up there with all this fire burning all around them." Although Leper is not able to make out who was who, he is able to say that that the person nearest the trunk of the tree bent his knees and pumped the branch in a pistonlike motion, causing the one out on the limb to fall. It is now clear to Phineas what happened, and he flees Assembly Hall, as if trying to evade the truth with a desperate physical gesture that would shake off the facts as he once shook off tacklers. The sound of his body tumbling down the marble staircase tells the others that he has taken a second terrible fall.

There are several salient features in the final and climactic scene that closes Chapter 11. As elsewhere in the novel, Knowles has employed imagery to define the emotional condition and thematic implications of this crucial situation. We have already commented on the images of death and darkness associated with the courtroom setting, but the imagery used by Leper in his testimony draws comparisons between the boys in the tree and men at war. If one remembers the opening description of the tree, it was associated with warfare, looking "as forbidding as an artillery piece." Here Leper's impressionistic creation of the moment of Gene's crime employs more war imagery—the sun's rays "shooting like golden machine gun fire"—thus linking what happens between the boys in the tree with the hostility of nations at war with each other. . . .

Finny's Death Almost Inevitable

The cost of Gene's struggle for self-knowledge is extremely high, and the price for it is no less than Finny's life. Despite Dr. Stanpole's assurance that the injury to Finny's leg is a "clean break" and creating expectations that he will recover, when the leg is reset some bone marrow gets into the blood stream, and Finny dies of heart arrest. Trying to communicate his sympathy to Gene, the doctor explains: "There are risks, there are always risks. . . . An operating room and a war" are much the same he suggests.

As unexpected as Finny's death is to the reader, it has been anticipated by Knowles and is indeed almost inevitable. The symbolism of Finny's broken heart is inescapable. He did not have the heart to keep up the illusion of the world that had sustained him. Finny's death is also necessary for Gene to achieve his eventual separate peace and to accept the understanding of himself that he learned from Finny. When Gene says that he did not weep at Finny's funeral, it is because he does not feel separated from his friend but instead feels so fully integrated that he says, "I could not escape a feeling that this was my own funeral, and you do not cry in that case."

Generational Differences

In the last chapter Knowles moves the plot forward several months to June 1943, when the class graduates. His purpose for extending the story beyond the dramatic point of Finny's death is to introduce the war theme again and to sound the generation gap motif. To do so he brings in a new character, Brinker's father, a World War I veteran whose "Nathan Hale" patriotism is offensive to both his son and Gene. His view of war is analogous to preparing one's résumé. Combat duty, according to Mr. Hadley, will provide war memories to reminisce about in future years as they recall their heroic youth in the marines, paratroops, or as frogmen [navy divers]. To Brinker and Gene the prospect of risking their lives in order to have some future bragging rights is totally unrealistic. Much to Mr. Hadley's dismay, Gene tells him he is going into the navy to avoid fighting in foxholes with the infantry; Brinker's plan is to join the coast guard because he hopes it will be a safer service. The scene, which is one of the only extended depictions of parents, with the exception of Leper's mother, is intended to draw a distinction between the older and younger generations. Paradoxically, the boys conclude that the World War I generation is childish and that they are the mature ones. Their disillusionment is akin to Finny's view, who maintained that the war was a joke that fat and foolish old men played on younger men. However, Gene forms an independent idea. To him, "it seemed clear that wars were made not by generations and their special stupidities, but that wars were made instead by something ignorant in the human heart."

Gene Makes Peace with Himself

The last pages of the novel serve to extend Gene's awareness as narrator beyond the moment in time that he is located and to assure us that he has reached the point of understanding his experiences. This part of the novel thus forms a kind of coda [addendum] that conveys Knowles's evaluation of the book's meaning.

Gene's recovery and reintegration, which will cure his alienation and "double vision," depend upon a process of spiritual symbiosis. Those qualities in Finny that were most vital and life-giving are assumed by Gene, while the negative traits are exorcised by Finny's death. Gene's psyche is integrated and harmonized by the forgiveness and love that Finny extended to his friend. Thus, a transfigured Gene faces life in an atmosphere Phineas created, "sizing up the world with erratic and entirely personal reservations, letting its rocklike facts sift through and be accepted only a little at a time ...". In an estimate of Finny's character that is reminiscent of [F. Scott Fitzgerald's] *The Great Gatsby*, Knowles writes, "He possessed an extra vigor, a heightened confidence in himself, a serene capacity for affection which saved him ... Nothing even about the war had broken his harmonious and natural unity." Paradoxically, as Gene listens to an army drill instructor calling cadence, he involuntarily gets into step with the count, in a way anticipating his transformation into military life. He says that "later under the influence of an even louder voice ... I fell into step as well as my nature, Phineas-filled, would allow."

Finny's friendship has taught Gene that instinctive and impulsive reactions to life need not be evil or savage. His life offered Gene the example of a positive possibility, an ideal of conduct that he can commit himself to follow. So when Gene goes off to the war, he goes without any hatred, and he never kills anyone because, as he says, "he has already killed his enemy"—meaning that he has eliminated self-ignorance, which was his real enemy. Thus, he has made a separate peace, and war within himself, which he had waged at such a high cost, is finally over.

A *Separate Peace* Addresses the Moral Effect of World War II on American Society

James L. McDonald

James L. McDonald was an assistant professor of English at the University of Detroit.

Knowles writes in the tradition of the American "novel of manners," along with F. Scott Fitzgerald and Henry James, according to McDonald in the following essay. A Separate Peace is concerned with the impact of war on the hearts and minds of the young men who are not yet involved in battle, but who know they will soon be participants. Like James, Knowles uses the device of the unreliable narrator—Gene Forrester's version of events is open to other interpretations. McDonald argues that although Knowles is not a writer of the stature of James, A Separate Peace reveals him as a skillful, promising young author who has successfully tackled important themes.

It may be too early to attempt more than a tentative appraisal of the overall achievement of John Knowles. Certainly one can say that he ranks among the most promising young American novelists; and one can recognize the obvious fact that *A Separate Peace* . . . has become a small classic among college students and seems likely to last for some time. His other novels, however, have only been noticed in passing: *Morning in Antibes* and *Indian Summer* have not really been analyzed and evaluated. Nor is there any substantial critical commentary on Knowles's work as a whole.

James L. McDonald, "The Novels of John Knowles," *Arizona Quarterly*, vol. 23, Winter 1967, pp. 335–37, 341–42. Copyright © 1967 by the Regents of the University of Arizona. Reproduced by permission of the publisher and the author.

Novels of Manners

I would like to begin such a commentary; and I propose to do so by *placing* Knowles, as it were—by relating him to the American literary tradition which I see him working within. He is writing what [literary critic] Lionel Trilling has called "the novel of manners"; and it seems to me that there are affinities between his aesthetic preoccupations and those of Henry James and F. Scott Fitzgerald. An examination of his subjects, themes, and techniques should show this affinity; and I hope that it will also provide a basis for a reasonably sound estimate of Knowles's stature as a novelist.

From the beginning of his career, Knowles—like James and Fitzgerald—has written about manners, about what Trilling defines as "a culture's hum and buzz of implication . . . the whole evanescent context in which its explicit statements are made." In Knowles's first novel, *A Separate Peace* (New York, 1959), the "explicit statements" are the Second World War and its moral effect on American society; the "context" is made up of the precarious situation of American prep-school students who will soon be combatants, and of the moral responses that they, their teachers, and their parents make to this situation.

The Impact of War on Individuals

As many critics have noted, *A Separate Peace* can be viewed as a war novel, drawing its title from Frederic Henry's personal declaration of personal armistice in [Ernest Hemingway's] *A Farewell to Arms*. Knowles's concern, however, is not with the direct confrontation of the obvious realities of the battlefield; rather, it is with the impact of war on the minds and sensibilities of individuals who are not, as yet, immediately involved. The novel examines the cultural upheaval created by the war, and shows how the resulting moral climate affects the thoughts, feelings, attitudes, and actions of Gene Forrester, Phineas, Leper, Brinker, and the others. The novel deals, then, with culture, and with the sensibility of the individual as it is formed by a particular culture: like James and Fitzgerald, Knowles draws the reader's attention to the individual's efforts to adjust to cultural change, and to the quality of his moral responses as he attempts to cope with the disruption of his formerly stable world.

Particularly Jamesian in this novel is Knowles's use of point of view. The narrator, the principal character, is Gene Forrester. On the surface, it appears that he is telling his story honestly, attempting to grapple with his past and forthrightly informing the reader of its significance. Yet, like the narrators of James's "The Liar" or *The Aspern Papers*, for example, Forrester frequently seems either unaware of or deliberately unwilling to acknowledge the moral nature and consequences of his attitudes and actions. There is, then, a discrepancy between Forrester's judgments and the actions and attitudes he is judging. The reader's awareness of this discrepancy is enforced by the dramatic statements of other characters in the novel, especially by the comments of Leper.

Thus the reader's judgments are not always the same as the narrator's; and so the reader is led to question the narrator's motives and interpretations. Should Forrester be taken at his own evaluation? Or is he really, as Leper charges, "a savage underneath" his pose of refined, dispassionate, reflective survivor and recounter of the ordeal?

Knowles Owes a Debt to James

The complexity—or the ambiguity—of the novel is precisely here, and so is Knowles's debt to James. Neither novelist merely uses his narrator to direct the narrative. Both, instead, use the narrative as the scene and occasion of a complex, dramatic confrontation between the narrator and his past which the reader participates in. For James and Knowles, the aesthetic effect of this type of novel depends on a dramatic interplay between the narrator's judgments and the reader's; and, in this sense, the narrator *is* the story. . . .

It would be foolish, of course, to claim that Knowles belongs in the select company of Fitzgerald and James, to contend that *Morning in Antibes* and *Indian Summer* are comparable in quality to [Fizgerald's] *Tender Is The Night* and [James's] *The Ambassadors*. But I think that he is an enormously promising novelist, and that he has already achieved a genuine stature. He has exhibited the courage to tackle large subjects and significant themes; and he has treated them with taste, understanding, and considerable technical skill. He certainly deserves more attention than he has received up until now.

Devon School Is a Microcosm of a World at War

Wiley Lee Umphlett

Wiley Lee Umphlett taught sociology at the University of West Florida for more than twenty-five years. He is the author of Creating the Big Game.

Both A Separate Peace *and Mark Harris's* Bang the Drum Slowly *use the metaphor of the athlete dying young to address the theme of individuality, contends Umphlett in the following article. Both works deal with the friendship of two young men, one of whom is an athlete who dies at a young age. In both cases, the survivor gains self-knowledge as a result of the death of his friend. With World War II lurking in the future for his two students, Knowles uses the sporting myth to advance his theme that the same predilection for evil that causes animosity among schoolboys is also responsible for war.*

The aura of innocence surrounding the traditional figure of the sporting myth is compellingly dramatized through the image of the dying athlete in both John Knowles's *A Separate Peace* (1959) and Mark Harris's *Bang the Drum Slowly* (1956). The predicament of dying young when contrasted with the sporting hero's quest for immortality is strikingly used in these novels to comment on the meaning of individuality in our day. In both works this definition grows out of the interrelationship of their two main characters—that between Gene and Phineas in *A Separate Peace* and Henry Wiggen and Bruce Pearson in *Bang the Drum Slowly*. In both novels, too, the death of one character results in self-knowledge for the other, who in both cases happens to be the narrator. While Gene

Forrester gains a fuller understanding of the evil that separates man from man, Henry Wiggen acquires a greater respect for the worth and dignity of the individual.

Metaphor of Sport Advances Plot

Essential encounter in *A Separate Peace*, while set against the larger background of World War II, focuses on the minor wars declared among the schoolboys of Devon, a prominent New England preparatory school, in order to explain the larger question of why wars come about. The friendship between Gene and Phineas, two offsetting personalities in that the former is a superior student and the latter an accomplished athlete, is eventually disrupted by what at first appears to be a trifling incident but is later expanded to support the novel's inherent theme: wars are caused by "something ignorant in the human heart."

In schoolboy literature related to the sporting myth, the major conflict exists between the ivory tower [of academia] and the playing field [of sport], or authority and self-expression; thus much of the significance of *A Separate Peace* is projected through the imagery and metaphor of the game. It is appropriate to observe here, too, that because they provide opportunity for self-expression, the playing fields of Devon are equated with the traditional wilderness of the sporting myth. As Gene informs us near the beginning of the novel:

> Beyond the gym and the fields began the woods, our, the Devon School's woods, which in my imagination were the beginning of the great northern forests. I thought that, from the Devon Woods, trees reached in an unbroken, widening corridor so far to the north that no one had ever seen the other end, somewhere up in the far unorganized tips of Canada. We seemed to be playing on the tame fringe of the last and greatest wilderness. I never found out whether this is so and perhaps it is.

The playing field as representative of the forest in microcosm becomes the great, good place, or the "last and greatest wilderness," where the inherent innocence of Phineas can find true expression. As Gene sees it, Finny believed that

> "you always win at sports." This "you" was collective. Everyone always won at sports. . . . Finny never permitted himself to realize that when you won they lost. That would have destroyed the perfect beauty which was sport. Nothing bad ever happened in sports; they were the absolute good.

The game of blitzball, which Finny himself invents to perk up a dull summer at Devon, is more than an example of his ingratiating manner with his fellow students; the game is a symbol of his very being:

> He had unconsciously invented a game which brought his own athletic gifts to their highest pitch. The odds were tremendously against the ball carrier, so that Phineas was driven to exceed himself practically everyday when he carried the ball. To escape the wolf pack which all the other players became he created reverses and deceptions and acts of sheer mass hypnotism which were so extraordinary that they surprised even him; after some of these plays I would notice him chuckling quietly to himself, in a kind of happy disbelief.

Experience Leads to Loss of Innocence

Phineas has [an Ernest] Hemingwaylike devotion to enjoyment of sporting endeavor as a thing in itself. His breaking a school swimming record and not reporting his feat for the record emphasize both his uniqueness as an individual and his role as a type of the sporting hero, in that to Phineas the pursuit is more important than the goal. But his athletic accomplishments also add to the fear already present in the inner being of Gene, his roommate, and his best friend. Gene tells himself: "You and Phineas . . . are even in enmity. You are both coldly driving ahead for yourselves alone." But the inter-

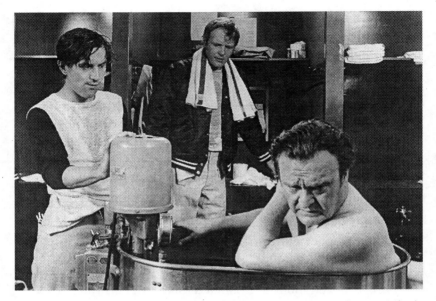

As in John Knowles's novel A Separate Peace, *Mark Harris's novel* Bang the Drum Slowly *(pictured in this movie still) uses the metaphor of a young, dying athlete to deal with the theme of individuality.* © Bettmann/Corbis.

relationship of both characters is structured to bring about the novel's tragic denouement and dramatize its basic theme.

As the story develops, Gene's gnawing but unfounded fear that Phineas, out of envy, is seeking to destroy his reputation as a student causes him to mistake Phineas's real intentions. The upshot of this is a betrayal by Gene that results eventually in the death of Phineas but ultimately in the self-education of Gene. The Super Suicide Society of the Summer Session is another one of Finny's improvisations that not only brings out his athletic ability but also further endears himself to his adventure-starved classmates. To become a member of this "secret" organization one must merely leap from a tree limb that hangs treacherously over the river skirting the Devon campus. But Finny, ever the daredevil, proposes that he and Gene jump together. Gene, for some unaccountable reason, which he later explains to Phineas as "just some ignorance inside me, some crazy thing inside me, something blind," jounces the limb, causing Finny to fall to earth and break a leg. Still the innocent, Phineas, even though now physically through with sports, vicariously continues to identify with the sporting encounter through Gene: "Listen, pal, if *I* can't play sports, you're going to play them for me." To which command Gene feels that "I lost part of myself to him then . . . this must have been my purpose from the first: to become a part of Phineas."

If, like many another figure in American literature, Phineas becomes a victim of his own innocence, then Gene, through his confrontation with the force of evil, gains self-knowledge at the expense of his own happiness, a state symbolized by his former relationship with Phineas. A dominant theme in our literature, the death of innocence results from the growth of experience. From the time of breaking his leg on, Phineas's existence, both physically and symbolically, becomes a slow death; and as Gene progresses in self-knowledge, Phineas diminishes in force as individual while increasing as image and symbol. A central trait of Gene's makeup is revealed when he says:

> I was used to finding something deadly in things that attracted me; there was always something deadly lurking in anything I wanted, anything I loved. And if it wasn't there, as for example with Phineas, then I put it there myself.

Contrast this outlook with that of Phineas, who, Gene observes, is "a poor deceiver, having had no practice," and in whom there "was no conflict except between athletes, something Greek-inspired and Olympian in which victory would go to whoever was the strongest in body and heart." In becoming a part of Phineas, though, Gene is made more aware of the difference between his own nature and Finny's, of the distinction between good and evil, of the contrast between illusion and reality.

Phineas, then, is the incarnation of the sporting hero before the fall, and in his world of the game there is no reminder of the real war going on in the outside world. When he is training Gene in his place for the '44 Olympics, Finny refutes Gene's observation that there will be no Olympics in 1944 with: "Leave your fantasy life out of this. We're grooming you for the Olympics, pal, in 1944." Phineas's flat denial of a schoolmaster's remark that "Games are all right in their place ... but all exercise today is aimed of course at the approaching Waterloo" is not only indicative of his natural antipathy toward the authoritarian attitude of the academician, but also exemplifies his philosophy of a world without war or, in effect, a world of Edenic innocence. Perhaps the one activity in the novel that best illustrates Phineas's special genius for maintaining his sense of the way the world should be is his organization of a winter carnival, a kind of comic bacchanal performed in the dead of the New England winter. Because of it, Gene tells us that a "liberation" had been "torn from the gray encroachments of 1943, that an escape had been concocted, this afternoon of momentary, illusory, special and separate peace." In this womanless world of the Devon School for boys, Phineas's outlook asserts that the innocent state can be retained for as long as one can separate self from the man-made or obligatory realities that engulf it. However, Knowles implies that the seeds of discord are inherent in man, and we sense that it is only a matter of time before Finny's ideal world will be destroyed.

Paradoxically, it is Leper Lepellier's departure as "the Devon School's first recruit to World War II" that serves as the catalyst for Gene's encounter with self and prepares the way for the novel's denouement. Leper, viewed as an oddball by his classmates, is a romantic who finds personal identification with the simple realities of nature. Thus he is easily persuaded by a recruiting movie about the ski troops that at least one area of the war experience has its fine moments. However, Leper's sensitivity is undermined by his contact with the military, and after fleeing this alien existence for the security of his Vermont home, he sends for Gene, a friend he believes he can confide in. Now, though, with a more realistic perspective on life, Leper is moved to remind Gene of his evil act: "'You always were a savage underneath. I always knew that only I never admitted it. . . . Like a savage underneath . . . like that time you knocked Finny out of the tree.'" Leper, once an innocent himself, can now recognize evil for what it is, and Gene, although fearful of the truth, in yet another step toward self-awareness must return to Devon and Phineas to discover it for himself. Phineas, still holding onto his "separate peace," reveals to Gene an even more heightened contrast between illusion and reality. As Gene says:

> I found Finny beside the woods playing and fighting—the two were approximately the same thing to him—and I stood there wondering whether things weren't simpler and better at the northern terminus of these woods, a thousand miles due north into the wilderness, somewhere deep into the Arctic, where the peninsula of trees which began at Devon would end at last in an untouched grove of pine, austere and beautiful.

Phineas Unprepared for Real World

Once again the sporting figure is identified with the primal virtues of the wilderness, and standing on the edge of Finny's snowball fight, Gene is hesitant as to which side to join, his outlook reflecting his present state of being—a Hegelian [after German philosopher Georg W.F. Hegel's theory of idealism] sense of self-alienation in which a dialectical development controls the individual consciousness and its progress from innocence to maturity. Having become increasingly aware of two antithetical ways of looking at experience, Gene, at this point, can say of his own experience that he no longer needed a "false identity; now I was acquiring, I felt, a sense of my own real authority and worth, I had had many new experiences and I was growing up." Now, "growing up" demands the renunciation of the illusory world of the child, and in terms of Gene's new experience, Phineas and what he stands for must "die." During a secret court in which Gene is placed on trial, the truth of what actually happened in the tree is about to be revealed, but Finny, in one last effort to cling to the significance of his world, rushes from the room, falls down a flight of stairs, and reinjures his leg. Complications set in, and a few days later he is dead.

The death of Phineas is necessary to Gene's experience, because, even though Phineas had thought of Gene as an "extension of himself," Gene's contact with the real facts of existence compels a break with the way of life Phineas represents. As Gene puts it concerning Phineas's funeral: "I could not escape a feeling that this was my own funeral, and you do not cry in that case." The death of innocence—the world of illusion and Edenic reverie—has instilled in Gene a new way of "seeing." After one of his last talks with Phineas, Gene feels that he now has to "cope with something that might be called double vision," since the familiar objects of the campus have taken on a different appearance:

> I saw the gym in the glow of a couple of outside lights near it and I knew of course that it was the Devon gym which I entered every day. It was and it wasn't. There was something innately strange about it, as though there had always been an inner core to the gym which I had never perceived before, quite different from its generally accepted appearance. It seemed to alter moment by moment before my eyes, becoming for brief flashes a totally unknown building with a significance much deeper and far more real than any I had noticed before . . . and under the pale night glow the playing fields swept away from me in slight frosty undulations which bespoke meanings upon meanings, levels of reality I had never suspected before, a kind of thronging and epic grandeur which my superficial eyes and cluttered mind had been blind to before.

Gene's new vision now focuses on complexities where there had formerly been a simple plane of existence equated with the innocent world of sporting endeavor. With the death of Phineas, then, Gene's essential encounter is complete, and at the end of the story he tells us:

> I was ready for the war, now that I no longer had any hatred to contribute to it. My fury was gone, I felt it gone, dried up at the source, withered and lifeless. Phineas had absorbed it and taken it with him, and I was rid of it forever.

Phineas, whose special attitude would have made him a casualty, escapes the disintegrating effect of war, whether it be between individuals or nations, escapes even the fact of losing his basic innocence and growing into a Christian Darling, [character in Irwin Shaw's "The 80-Yard Run"] or a Rabbit Angstrom [character in John Updike's *Run, Rabbit, Run*]. The "separate peace" declared by Phineas is genuine, for as Gene observes in comparing Phineas with his other classmates:

> Only Phineas never was afraid, only Phineas never hated anyone. Other people experienced this fearful shock somewhere, this sighting of the enemy, and so began an obsessive labor of defense, began to parry the menace they saw facing them by developing a particular frame of mind.

In contrasting two complementary types of the sporting myth, *A Separate Peace* meaningfully dramatizes the dangers involved when the individual encounters this inner enemy, for it is a powerful and mysterious foe, one that demands a special kind of defense.

The Growth from Innocence into Adulthood in *A Separate Peace*

James Ellis

James Ellis was a professor of English at the University of North Carolina at Greensboro and Mount Holyoke College.

Knowles employs a masterly use of symbolism to structure his novel and chart the growth from innocence to experience in A Separate Peace, *according to Ellis in the following essay. Three distinct pairs of symbols are used—summer and winter, the Devon and Naguamsett rivers, and war and peace. War is ugly, and Phineas, with his purity of heart, is unable to comprehend or accept it. Gene at first wants to escape the ugliness of war, which is contrasted to the beauty and peace of Devon School. At the novel's end, however, Gene recognizes that the true ugliness springs from an evil within the human heart and that war is only one of the manifestations of that evil.*

To read *A Separate Peace* is to discover a novel which is completely satisfactory and yet so provocative that the reader wishes immediately to return to it. John Knowles' achievement is due, I believe, to his having successfully imbued his characters and setting with a symbolism that while informative is never oppressive. Because of this the characters and the setting retain both the vitality of verisimilitude and the psychological tension of symbolism.

Three Sets of Symbols Provide Structure

What happens in the novel is that Gene Forrester and Phineas, denying the existence of the Second World War as they enjoy the summer peace of Devon School, move gradually to

James Ellis, "*A Separate Peace*: The Fall from Innocence," *The English Journal*, vol. 53, no. 5, May 1964, pp. 313–18. Copyright © 1964 by the National Council of Teachers of English.

a realization of an uglier adult world—mirrored in the winter and the Naguamsett River—whose central fact is the war. This moving from innocence to adulthood is contained within three sets of interconnected symbols. These three—summer and winter; the Devon River and the Naguamsett River; and peace and war—serve as a backdrop against which the novel is developed, the first of each pair dominating the early novel and giving way to the second only after Gene has discovered the evil of his own heart.

The reader is introduced to the novel by a Gene Forrester who has returned to Devon after an absence of fifteen years, his intention being to visit the two sites which have influenced his life—the tree, from which he shook Finny to the earth, and the First Academy Building, in which Finny was made to realize Gene's act. After viewing these two scenes, a "changed" Gene Forrester walks through the rain, aware now that his victory over his internal ignorance is secure. With this realization Gene tells his story of a Devon summer session and its consequences.

Described as ". . . tremendous, an irate, steely black steeple," the tree is a part of the senior class obstacle course in their preparation for war and is the focal center of the first part of the novel. As the Biblical tree of knowledge it is the means by which Gene will renounce the Eden-like summer peace of Devon and, in so doing, both fall from innocence and at the same time prepare himself for the second world war. As in the fall of Genesis, there is concerning this tree a temptation.

Taunted by Phineas to jump from the tree, Gene says: "I was damned if I'd climb it. The hell with it." Aside from its obvious school boy appropriateness, his remark foreshadows his later fall. Standing high in the tree after surrendering to Finny's dare, Gene hears Finny, who had characterized his initial jump as his contribution to the war effort, reintroduce the war motif, saying: "When they torpedo the troopship, you can't stand around admiring the view. Jump!" As Gene hears these words, he wonders: "What was I doing up here anyway? Why did I let Finny talk me into stupid things like this? Was he getting some kind of hold over me?" Then as Gene jumps, he thinks: "With the sensation that I was throwing my life away, I jumped into space."

Phineas Represents Innocence

What Finny represents in Gene's temptation is the pure spirit of man (mirrored in the boy Finny) answering its need to share the experience of life and innocent love. For Finny the war and the tree, which represents a training ground for the war, are only boyish delights. The reality of war is lost upon him because he is constitutionally pure and incapable of malice. That this is so can be seen from Gene's later statement regarding Finny as a potential soldier. He says:

> They'd get you some place at the front and there'd be a lull in the fighting, and the next thing anyone knew you'd be over with the Germans or the Japs, asking if they'd like to field a baseball team against our side. You'd be sitting in one of their command posts, teaching them English. Yes, you'd get confused and borrow one of their uniforms, and you'd lend them one of yours. Sure, that's just what would happen. You'd get things so scrambled up nobody would know who to fight any more. You'd make a mess, a terrible mess, Finny, out of the war.

The tragedy of the novel ultimately is that Gene is not capable of maintaining the spiritual purity that distinguishes Phineas and so must as he discovers his own savagery betray Phineas.

Once the two jumps have been effected, a bond has been cemented between the two. But as Gene and Finny walk up to the dormitories, Gene forgets that he has, in following Finny, denied the adult rules which regulate human relationships, and lapses back into his concern for authority. Falling into his "West Point stride," he says: "We'd better hurry or we'll be late for dinner." Phineas, however, objects to Gene's having forgot-

ten what is exemplified in the jumping from the tree and trips
Gene. After a brief scuffle the two boys resume their walk.
Gene, then, acknowledges that he has succumbed to Finny. He
says:

> Then Finny trapped me again in his strongest trap, that is, I
> suddenly became his collaborator. As we walked rapidly
> along, I abruptly resented the bell and my West Point stride
> and hurrying and conforming. Finny was right.

To acknowledge visibly his giving up the rules of Devon, Gene
now trips Finny, and the two are united in a boy's conspiracy
to elude adulthood and its rules.

Gene Grows to Envy Phineas

The progress of the novel after this joining of Phineas and
Gene is the progress of Gene's growing envy of Finny. Incapable of the spiritual purity of Phineas, Gene finds himself
jealous of Finny's ability to flout Devon rules in his quest to
enjoy an "unregulated friendliness" with the adult world. Gene
says apropos of several incidents involving Finny and the Devon rules:

> I was beginning to see that Phineas could get away with
> anything. I couldn't help envying him that a little, which
> was perfectly normal. There was no harm in envying even
> your best friend a little.

and

> This time he wasn't going to get away with it. I could feel
> myself becoming unexpectedly excited at that.

And when Finny does evade punishment, Gene thinks:

> He had gotten away with everything. I felt a sudden stab of
> disappointment. That was because I just wanted to see some
> more excitement; that must have been it.

It is during a bicycle trip to the beach on the morning of
the day on which Gene will push Finny from the tree that

Finny confides to Gene that he is his best friend. Gene, however, cannot respond. He says: "I nearly did. But something held me back. Perhaps I was stopped by that level of feeling, deeper than thought, which contains the truth." The effect of this trip is to cause Gene to fail a trigonometry test and thereby to bring his hatred of Finny into the open. Inventing reasons to explain what exists only in his projecting it upon Phineas, Gene says as he realizes what he thinks is Finny's plot:

> Then a second realization broke. . . . Finny had deliberately set out to wreck my studies. . . . That way he, the great athlete, would be way ahead of me. It was all cold trickery, it was all calculated, it was all enmity.

Later, just before he will shake Finny from the tree, Gene confronts Phineas with his suspicions. Finny's surprise at the charge is such that Gene realizes its falsity. Confronted with the evident truth of Finny's denial, Gene understands his inferiority to Phineas and his own moral ugliness, made the more so when juxtaposed to Finny's innocence. It is this realization that prompts his conscious shaking of the tree, which casts Phineas to the earth and which serves as Gene's initiation into the ignorance and moral blackness of the human heart.

Gene Experiences the Loss of Innocence

Returning to the fall session without Phineas, Gene finds that peace has deserted Devon. And replacing the freedom of his careless summer are the rules of Devon, to which Gene now gives his allegiance.

Unable to take part in the boyish activities and sports of Devon because of his guilt, Gene attempts to find anonymity in a dead-end job as assistant crew manager. But here, confronted with the arrogance of Cliff Quackenbush (about whom there is an aura of undefined ugliness which separates him from the other boys), Gene is forced to defend Phineas from a slighting remark. This fight between Gene and Quackenbush concludes with their tumbling into the Naguamsett River.

Both the Naguamsett and the Devon flow through the grounds of the school; but it had been into the Devon, a familiar and bucolic river suggestive of Eden, that Finny and Gene had jumped from the tree. But after his fall from innocence, Gene experiences a baptism of a different sort as he plunges into the Naguamsett—a saline, marshy, ugly river "governed by unimaginable factors like the Gulf Stream, the Polar Ice Cap, and the moon."

In what Gene says after his fall into the Naguamsett is introduced the latter parts of the paired symbols that were discussed earlier—the winter, the Naguamsett, and the war (fight). Gene says of his fall:

> I had taken a shower to wash off the sticky salt of the Naguamsett River—going into the Devon was like taking a refreshing shower itself, you never had to clean up after it, but the Naguamsett was something else entirely. I had never been in it before; it seemed appropriate that my baptism there had taken place on the first day of this winter session, and that I had been thrown into it, in the middle of a fight.

And just as Gene has gone from the innocence exemplified in the Devon River to the experience of the Naguamsett, so the peaceful Devon River itself, whose course "was determined by some familiar hills a little inland" and which "rose among highland farms and forests," ultimately must succumb to the cosmic force of the world; for it, after passing "at the end of its course through the school grounds," then "threw itself with little spectacle over a small waterfall beside the diving dam, and into the turbid Naguamsett."

Gene Is Regenerated

The return of Phineas to Devon signals the rejuvenation and regeneration of Gene. Immediately prior to Finny's return, Gene had discovered in Brinker's announcement of his intention to enlist a chance to close the door on the pain that has haunted him since his crime against Finny. He says of enlistment and its offer to allow him to consecrate himself to the destruction of the war and to his own capacity for evil:

> To enlist. To slam the door impulsively on the past, to shed everything down to my last bit of clothing, to break the pattern of my life—that complex design I had been weaving alone since birth with all its dark threads, its unexplainable symbols set against a conventional background of domestic white and schoolboy blue, all those tangled strands which required the dexterity of a virtuoso to keep flowing—I yearned to take giant military shears to it, snap! bitten off in an instant, and nothing left in my hands but spools of khaki which could weave only plain, flat, khaki design, however twisted they might be.
>
> Not that it would be a good life. The war would be deadly all right. But I was used to finding something deadly in things that attracted me; there was something deadly lurking in anything I wanted, anything I loved. And if it wasn't there, as for example with Phineas, then I put it there myself.
>
> But in the war, there was no question about it at all; it was there.

But with Phineas' return and Gene's realization that Phineas needs him to help him maintain his integrity, Gene finds moral purpose and determines to live out his life at Devon with Finny. He says:

> Phineas was shocked at the idea of my leaving. In some way he needed me. He needed me. I was the least trustworthy person he had ever met. I knew that; he knew or should know that too. I had even told him. I had told him. But there was no mistaking the shield of remoteness in his face and voice. He wanted me around. The war then passed away from me, and dreams of enlistment and escape and a clean start lost their meaning for me.

With Gene's resolution, peace returns to Devon and the war is forgotten.

For Phineas, who had even before his fall denied the American bombing of Central Europe, the war is a make-believe—a rumor started by various villains who wish to keep the pure spirit of youth enslaved. Explaining to Gene his vision, Finny points to the roaring twenties "when they all drank bathtub gin and everybody who was young did just what they wanted," and then explains that "the preachers and the old ladies and all the stuffed shirts" stepped in and tried to stop it with Prohibition. But everyone got drunker so they then arranged the depression to keep "the people who were young in the thirties in their places." And when they found "they couldn't use that trick forever," they "cooked up this war fake" for the forties, the *they* now being "the fat old men who don't want us crowding them out of their jobs."

What is important in Finny's theory is that it makes of the war an adult device which curtails the enjoyment of youth and its gifts. To accept the war is for Finny to accept a fallen world. So persuasive is his own illusion and his own magnetic power that Gene is momentarily caught up in it and can deny the war, the denial, however, being occasioned not so much by Finny's explanation as it is by Gene's "own happiness" in having momentarily evaded the ugliness of the war.

The Phineas-inspired Devon Winter Carnival is the occasion during which Gene is to be paraded in all his Olympic glory, signifying that he, through consecrating himself to Finny's tutelage, has become like Phineas. About this winter carnival and his brilliant decathlon performance, Gene says:

> It wasn't the cider which made me surpass myself, it was this liberation we had torn from the gray encroachments of 1943, the escape we had concocted, this afternoon of momentary, illusory, special and separate peace.

Yet even as this illusion is achieved, a telegram arrives from Leper, an "escapee" from the war, come back to destroy Gene's illusion of withdrawing from the war.

At Leper's home in Vermont, Gene finds himself accused of having been responsible for Finny's fall. Later, after the heat of the accusation has passed, the two boys walk in the snow-covered fields while Leper reveals the horror of the military. As he talks, Gene hears the "frigid trees . . . cracking with the cold." To his ears they sound "like rifles being fired in the distance." This paralleling of the trees (the scene of Gene's fall in particular and nature in general) with the war (and hence the ignorance of human heart, which is responsible for both war and private evil) is given reverberation at Gene's inquisition when Leper describes Gene and Finny as they stood in the tree just before Finny's fall. To Leper they looked "black as death with this fire [the sun] burning all around them; and the rays of the sun were shooting past them, millions of rays shooting past them like—like golden machine-gun fire." Nature then is presented as both damned and damning, with man's death and fall insured by nature's deadly fire and by his own inability to escape the savage within himself.

For Gene, as he listens to Leper, the ugliness of the war finally becomes so forceful that he must run, saying as he does: "I didn't want to hear any more about it. . . . Not now or ever. I didn't care because it had nothing to do with me. And I didn't want to hear any more of it. Ever."

What Gene wants is to return to the world of the winter carnival and his training for the Olympics, his and Phineas' withdrawal from the ugliness of the world. He says:

> I wanted to see Phineas, and Phineas only. With him there was no conflict except between athletes, something Greek-inspired and Olympian in which victory would go to who-ever was the strongest in body and heart. This was the only conflict he had ever believed in.

Gene Gains Self-Knowledge

The reconciliation of Gene and Finny after Finny's refusal to accept Brinker's "f___ing facts" and his fall provides the culmination of the novel. Questioned by Finny, Gene denies that his pushing of Phineas was personal. Beginning to understand himself, Gene says: "It was just some ignorance inside me, some crazy thing inside me, something blind, that's all." And joined with this realization is Gene's admission that war, despite Phineas, does exist and that it grows out of the ignorance of the human heart. In rejecting Brinker's thesis that wars can be laid to one's parents and their generation, Gene says: "... It seemed clear that wars were not made by generations and their special stupidities, but that wars were made instead by something ignorant in the human heart." Gene has discovered that his private evil, which caused him to hurt Phineas, is the same evil—only magnified—that results in war.

Finny alone, Gene now knows, was incapable of malice. Reviewing his relation with Phineas, Gene tells of Finny's way "of sizing up the world with erratic and entirely personal reservations, letting its rocklike facts sift through and be accepted only a little at a time, only as much as he could assimilate without a sense of chaos and loss."

Because of his ability to admit only as much of the ugliness of life as he could assimilate, Phineas was unique. Gene says:

> No one else I have ever met could do this. All others at some point found something in themselves pitted violently against something in the world around them. With those of my year this point often came when they grasped the fact of the war. When they began to feel that there was this overwhelmingly hostile thing in the world with them, then the simplicity and unity of their characters broke and they were not the same again.

> Phineas alone had escaped this. He possessed an extra vigor, a heightened confidence in himself, a serene capacity for af-

fection which saved him. Nothing as he was growing up at home, nothing at Devon, nothing even about the war had broken his harmonious and natural unity. So at last I had.

It is because of his having known and loved Phineas that Gene can recognize that hatred springs from a greater evil that is within. It is the realization of this that releases him from the hysteria of the war, which now moves from its controlling position off-stage onto the campus of Devon in the form of the parachute riggers.

Unlike his friends who had sought through some building of defenses to ward off the inevitability of evil, Gene has come to see that this enemy never comes from without, but always from within. He knows, moreover, that there is no defense to be built, only an acceptance and purification of oneself through love. Such a love did he share with Phineas in a private gypsy summer. And it is because of the purity of this love that he is able to survive his fall from innocence.

A *Separate Peace* Addresses Coming of Age During Wartime

Thomas Reed Whissen

Thomas Reed Whissen is a professor of English emeritus at Wright State University and the author of The Devil's Advocates.

A Separate Peace *has achieved cult status because it is the best version of a novel dealing with coming of age in a prep school setting to be written by an American, according to Whissen in the following article. Adolescence is a difficult time, but growing to maturity during wartime presents unique pressures, the author contends. There are several wars waging in the book— World War II in the background, Gene's conflict with Finny, and Gene's internal conflict about coming to terms with a world at war and the evil in his own heart.*

A Separate Peace may not be in a class by itself, but within the genre of novels about adolescent male friendships, it stands out from the others for reasons that are not immediately apparent. Like J.D. Salinger's *The Catcher in the Rye*, its popularity has not diminished since its original publication; it has never gone out of print, and it continues to sell at a steady pace. But more than that, it continues to exert a powerful influence on the young people who read it. The reasons for the success of this type of story are fairly predictable, but the singular success of this particular version of a familiar conflict bears closer scrutiny.

One possible reason for its special status in the United States is that it is easily the best version of this story written by an American. For this reason, young American readers can identify more closely with it than they can with the conventional English "public school" version, or with such foreign classics of the genre as Thomas Mann's *Tonio Kröger* or Hermann Hesse's *Narcissus and Goldmund.* Although the latter is familiar to many American readers, much of its popularity is owing to the cult status of its author, whose best-known books, namely *Steppenwolf, Demian,* and *Siddhartha,* have become such classics in themselves that his other works are relegated to a lower tier.

A Private and a Public War

As with *The Catcher in the Rye, A Separate Peace* reveals the loneliness of an adolescent boy attempting to come to terms with the world and with himself. Although both novels deal with prep school life and take place at about the same time, the differences are more significant than the similarities. Holden Caulfield [in *The Catcher in the Rye*] may be a child of the forties, but there is no mention in his story of war or of anything going on outside the small, stifling world Holden inhabits. In *A Separate Peace,* Gene Forrester's inner turmoil is set within the framework of the turmoil of World War II.

It is difficult enough to grow up during ordinary times when society is relatively stable, but when this maturing process takes place during a time of war, the instability of society only aggravates the insecurities that torment the adolescent mind. Gene Forrester is fighting his own private war. He is torn between remaining within the safety and seclusion of Devon School or abandoning this security for the confusion of the adult world. At the same time he is struggling to resist the influence of his best friend, Finny, and his undisciplined approach to life. Throughout the novel, Gene is tormented by the tensions within himself, by the conflict between him and Finny, and by the growing awareness of the unreal world of Devon School in contrast to a world at war.

The Enemy Is Within

Gene Forrester is a character whose worst enemy is himself. Although he is a capable athlete and an excellent student, Forrester is unable to prevent the dark side of his inner self from perverting and distorting his enjoyment of the world and the people around him. Like Holden Caulfield, Forrester always finds something bad in the things around him, and if he does not find it, he invents it. It is a paranoid proclivity that speaks to the reader—especially the young, impressionable reader—whose trust in those around him has been shaken or even shattered.

At one point in the novel, Gene is convinced that Finny is out to get him, that he is deliberately trying to destroy Gene's scholastic success. Since in reality Finny is totally indifferent to Gene's academic ambitions, there is no foundation for this suspicion; but Gene harbors it anyway because he would rather imagine Finny as a rival than accept that he really does not care. Like an abused child who prefers being beaten to being ignored, Gene prefers Finny's rivalry (even if imaginary) to his indifference. This is a feeling cult readers respond to completely, for if there is one fear that is common to most adolescents, it is the fear of being ignored. Recognition they crave, of course; rejection they can handle; but to be treated as if they did not exist, especially by someone they admire or love, is torment beyond endurance.

Once he has convinced himself of Finny's perfidy, Gene decides that he must somehow get even. He does this by causing Finny to fall from a tree and break a leg. The tree is no ordinary tree; it is a special tree that the schoolboys like to climb to jump into the river. Gene and Finny are the youngest ever to try this feat, and once they succeed, Finny organizes the Summer Suicide Society, whose sole purpose is to initiate new members by having them jump into the river. At each initiation, Gene and Finny jump first, but Gene never loses his fear of jumping. Near the end of summer, under pressure of exams and the growing conviction that Finny is undermining his scholastic endeavors, Gene jumps up and down on a limb, causing Finny to fall and break a leg. As it turns out, the leg is so shattered that Finny may not walk again, let alone participate in any sport.

At first Finny refuses to think that Gene had anything to do with the accident, even after Gene confesses. Eventually, there is an inquiry into the matter, and as he sees Gene being accused, Finny leaves the assembly room in a state of extreme agitation. He is so upset that he falls down the stairs and breaks the same leg again. When Gene appears at his bedside the following day, Finny has come to realize that Gene did indeed cause him to fall from the tree, and he asks Gene why. Gene is powerless to explain, blaming it on some mysterious blind impulse. But cult readers know, and their anguish is for the feeling between the two boys that cannot be expressed. And when, a short time later, marrow gets into Finny's bloodstream and he dies suddenly, Gene grieves but does not cry, for he feels that he, too, has died and that it is not fitting to cry over one's own death.

A Complex Relationship

The loss of a friend through one's own excessive feeling is a common adolescent misfortune. It is fraught with irony, for the ultimate loss is precipitated by the fear of loss. How, one asks, do I hang on to this friend whom I love more than he loves me? If he should die, then he would never leave, and I could carry with me the melancholy memory of a friendship frozen in time. To be responsible for the death of that friend is closer to suicide than to murder—at least in the mind of the tormented one. Like some sort of weird reworking of *Romeo and Juliet*, the two star-crossed friends find peace in the permanence of death. In this case, however, the one responsible for the accident lives on, unpunished except by his own guilt, a guilt he aggravates into an abiding pain that sustains him the way mortification of the flesh sustains the flagellant [one who whips the body to discipline it].

The relationship between Gene and Finny is representative of the sort of symbiotic relationship to be found in much modern literature including many cult novels. Mann deals with it definitively in *Tonio Kröger*, and it is prominent in several of the Hesse novels mentioned earlier. There are reminders of it in the contrasting personalities to be found within the gangs in S.E. Hinton's *The Outsiders*, in Anthony Burgess's *A Clockwork Orange*, and Oakley Hall's *Warlock*. There is even a hint of it in the teacher/learner relationship in Carlos Castaneda's *The Teaching of Don Juan*, and more than a hint of it in the mutually destructive relationship between Hunter Thompson and his Samoan lawyer in *Fear and Loathing in Las Vegas*.

In these relationships, one person usually symbolizes what the other person wants to be. Emil Sinclair wants to be Demian, Tonio Kröger wants to be Hans Hansen, and Gene Forrester wants to be Finny. In mythology, the object of idealization is a god, and the only way to become that god is to overcome him, sacrifice him, devour him, symbolically cannibalize him. Christ on the cross is an enormously pathetic figure, but He is also a comforting one, for now the tables are turned, the Savior needs *our* protection, and at last we can unburden ourselves of an obligation too great to bear. This interpretation may seem extreme, but it is the only one that gets at the heart of a story in which one friend kills another out of love.

A Homoerotic Fantasy

Gene loves Finny so much that he must either become him or get rid of him. And since he cannot nail him to a cross and then partake of his flesh and blood, he must do away with him. Gene's suppressed homoerotic feelings only intensify his extreme idealization of the god Phineas. Finny is the guy who can do everything, can construct a world all his own out of his imagination. It is Finny who invents new games to play, and it is even Finny's idea to jump from the tree into the river. Finny is all spontaneity.

His one flaw—his tragic flaw, as it were—is that he cannot face unpleasant realities. It is the fate of most tragic heroes that they are blind to an essential truth, the very truth that eventually leads to their downfall. At the end of *A Separate Peace*, Finny is forced to confront the truth about Gene's perfidy, and he runs away from it. Dealing with this reality seems to break Finny's will at the novel's end. Of course, then, he must die. How could Gene stand it if Finny were to remain alive, remembering? Would Finny accuse him, forgive him, or, more likely, ignore him?

Finny's death is necessary to the novel, but it is also a dead giveaway. Beyond resolving the plot and concluding the story, it betrays a homosexual fantasy in which the beloved dies a young and tragic death, leaving the lover with a memory that is more secure than reality. This, then, is the separate peace that appeals to dreamy young readers half in love with the captain of the soccer team.

The finishing touch to this unsettling study in the labyrinths of adolescent psychology occurs at Finny's burial when Gene cannot cry because he has the feeling that part of himself is being buried with his friend. What is being buried, of course, is not just his guilt over Finny's death but the guilt he feels about those dark impulses that brought on his actions in the first place. When, later, Gene enlists and goes off to war, he does so without any strong feelings, almost as if his emotions have been anesthetized. In symbolically killing the enemy inside himself, he has effectually excised his capacity to feel anything at all. It is a curiously merciless resolution to the problem, as if the penitent, through pain and tribulation, has driven not only the devils into exile but the angels as well.

It is bitterly ironic that Gene's torment will be the awful torment of indifference, the very thing he most feared from Finny. For, as [poet] John Donne says, "When God's hand is bent to strike, 'it is a fearful thing to fall into the hands of the living God'; but to fall out of the hands of the living God is a horror beyond our expression, beyond our imagination."

A *Separate Peace* Shows That the Condition of Life Is War

Peter Wolfe

Peter Wolfe is Curators' Professor of English at the University of Missouri–St. Louis, a renowned literary critic and author, and an expert in American detective fiction.

The ideas of original sin and the inevitable presence of evil in the world are central to an understanding of A Separate Peace, *states Wolfe in the following article. Using images drawn from warfare, Knowles creates an atmosphere where violence and malevolence are ever-present, even in the seemingly bucolic and peaceful setting of Devon School. The games that Gene and Finny participate in are tinged with violence and presage the military action that presumably awaits them. The most treacherous enemies in* A Separate Peace *are best friends, Wolfe contends, proving that hate and evil are in the human heart.*

John Knowles's concern with morality colors all his books. This preoccupation finds its most general expression in a question asked in *Double Vision* (1964), an informal travel journal: "Can man prevail against the bestiality he himself has struggled out of by a supreme effort?" Knowles's novels, instead of attacking the question head-on, go about it indirectly. They ask, first, whether a person can detach himself from his background—his society, his tradition, and the primitive energies that shaped his life.

War Is Central to Life

The question is important because Knowles sees all of modern life shot through with malevolence. The sound the "frigid trees" make during a winter walk in *A Separate Peace* resembles

Peter Wolfe, "The Impact of Knowles's *A Separate Peace*," *The University Review*, vol. 36, March 1970, pp. 189–93, 197–98. Copyright © 1969 by The Curators of the University of Missouri. All rights reserved. Reproduced by permission of the author.

"rifles being fired in the distance"; later, a character likens the rays of the sun to a volley of machine-gun fire. The book cries to be read in the context of original sin: its central event of a character falling from a tree: the snakelike rush of sibilants in "The Super Suicide Society of the Summer Session," an informal daredevil club whose founding leads to the novel's tragedy: an ocean wave that "hissed . . . toward the deep water" after upending a character: the "dead gray waves hissing mordantly along the beach" the next day.

This universal implication in guilt makes good a major premise of Knowles's fiction: that the condition of life is war. *A Separate Peace* describes the private battles of a prep school coterie boiling into the public fury of World War II. . . .

The Knowles hero, rather than tearing himself from his background, submerges himself in it. According to Knowles, man can only know himself through action; he learns about life by acting on it, not by thinking about it. The action is never collective, and it always involves treachery and physical risk.

A full life to Knowles is one lived on the margins of disaster. Brinker Hadley in *A Separate Peace* and Neil Reardon in *Indian Summer* are both actionists, but since their lives are governed by prudence and not feeling, they can never probe the quick of being. In order to touch the spontaneous, irrational core of selfhood, man must act unaided. At this point Knowles's ontology [theory of being] runs into the roadblock of original sin. Whereas the characters in his books who shrink from a bone-to-bone contact with life are labelled either escapists or cowards, the ones who lunge headlong into reality are usually crushed by the reality they discover. That all of Knowles's leading characters smash their closest friendship and also fall sick conveys the danger of a highly charged encounter with life.

This danger increases because of the way they go about the problem of self-being. Instead of struggling out of bestiality, to use Knowles's metaphor from *Double Vision*, they sink back into it. The Knowles hero moves forward by moving backward. *A Separate Peace* mentions "the deep tacit way in which feeling becomes stronger than thought," "that level of feeling, deeper than thought, which contains the truth," and "that deep layer of the mind where all is judged by the five senses and primitive expectation."

Prime being, then, is both sensory and prereflective, a tremor of uncensored energy. By obeying this dark urgency we can unleash a wildness that cuts down everything in its path. Gene Forrester insists that his shaking of his best friend, Phineas, out of a tree was prompted by "some ignorance inside me"; later he says that "wars were made . . . by something ignorant in the human heart." The first movers of our consciousnesses are "ignorant" in that they override reason and order. But unless we give them full rein we can never unroll our energies full force.

Violence Coexists with Innocence

A Separate Peace shapes the problem of man's inherent savagery to American culture. In contrast to the characters of D.H. Lawrence, those of Knowles do not discharge their deepest impulses sexually. Instead they retrace the familiar American fictional pattern of immersing themselves in the past. But where [F. Scott] Fitzgerald's Gatsby [in *The Great Gatsby*] hankers after the glamor of first love and [Arthur] Miller's Willy Loman [in *Death of a Salesman*] looks back to the days when salesmanship was adventurous, Knowles's Gene Forrester reaches back much further. He sounds the uncharted seas of our common humanity and in so doing both undoes the work of civilization and reawakens the wild meaninglessness of primitive man.

The novel's setting gives Gene's problem an American emphasis. In *Double Vision*, Knowles discusses the primitive barbarism underlying American life: "The American character is unintegrated, unresolved, a careful Protestant with a savage stirring in his insides, a germ of American wildness thickening in his throat." This elemental threat, Knowles continues, is all the more lethal for being hidden: "American life has an orderly, rather dull and sober surface, but with something berserk stirring in its depths."

Devon School in New Hampshire, "the most beautiful school in New England" and a haven of gentility, sportsmanship, and academic honors, has the same sort of deceptiveness. Its tame surface and schoolboy remoteness from World War II make it an unlikely setting for violence. As he does with the smiling, boyish soldiers who appear in the last chapter of the novel, Knowles uses a prep school setting to show that even innocence and beauty cannot escape the corrosive ooze of evil. (Devon's Field House is called suggestively "The Cage," indicating that bestiality is already in force at the school.) Contributing to the irony established by the disjuncture of cause and effect, or setting and event, is Knowles's quiet, understated style. That violence should leap so suddenly out of Knowles's offhand, conversational cadences sharpens the horror of the violence. . . .

Gene Forrester Is Morally Ambiguous

The first chapter of *A Separate Peace* shows Gene Forrester returning to Devon fifteen years after the key incident of his life—that of shaking his best friend Phineas out of a tree and shattering his leg. Mingling memory and fear, Gene is not only the archetypal criminal who returns to the scene of his crime or the American fictional hero who retreats into a private past. His return to Devon is purposive, even compulsive. His neglecting to mention his job, his family, or his home suggests that he has none of these things, even though he is past the age of thirty. He relives his act of treachery and the events surrounding it in the hope of recovering the separate peace of the summer of 1942.

Gene interests us chiefly because of his moral ambiguity: whereas he accepts his malevolence, he also resists indulging it at the expense of others. Fear of unleashing his inherent wickedness explains his inertia since Devon's 1942–43 academic year. It also explains his psychological bloc. His first-person narration is laced with self-abuse, special pleading, flawed logic, and evasiveness. As has been suggested, self-exploration is dangerous work, and Gene cannot be blamed if he sometimes cracks under the strain. Out of joint with both himself and his time, he subjects to reason an area of being which is neither rational nor reducible to rational formulas. Although the sum will not add, he has no choice but to try to add the sum if he wants to re-enter the human community.

Like the novel's memoir technique, Gene Forrester's name certifies that *A Separate Peace* is his book. Of the forest, Gene is a primitive, bloodthirsty woodlander; his occasional self-disclosures spell out the urgency of his death-pull: "I was used to finding something deadly in things that attracted me; there was always something deadly lurking in anything I wanted, anything I loved. And if it wasn't there . . . I put it there myself."

The forest has negative associations throughout the book. At one point Gene is accused of undermining his health by "smoking like a forest fire." Elsewhere the forest is equated with the raw icy wilderness stretching from the northern edge of Devon School to "the far unorganized tips of Canada." As it is in [poet] Emily Dickinson, summer for Knowles is the time of flowing beauty and intensity of being. The Sommers family are the most vital characters in *Indian Summer*, and the gipsy spree of Gene and Phineas takes place during summer term.

Devon represents the last outpost of civilization to Gene. It wards off the primitive madness encroaching from the great northern forests, and it shields its students from the organized madness of World War II. Devon's 1942 summer term, the first in its history, is giving Gene and Phineas their last reprieve from a war-racked world. At sixteen, the boys and their classmates are the oldest students at Devon excused from taking both military subjects and preinduction physical exams.

In contrast to this freedom, winter brings loss, unreason, and hardness of heart. Nor is the heartless irrationality equated with Gene's forest background uncommon. His first name universalizes his glacial cruelty. While Phineas is a sport (who happens to excel in sports), Gene is generic, his barbarism deriving from his North American forebears. And the fact that he is a southerner shows how deeply this northern madness has bitten into American life.

The Tree Represents Life

The first object of Gene's return visit to Devon is the tree he ousted Phineas from fifteen years before. [Literary critic] James Ellis places the tree in a Christian context by calling it "the Biblical tree of knowledge." His interpretation is amply justified by parallels between the novel and orthodox Christianity: everything in the boys' lives changes for the worst after the tree incident, the tree and Christ's crucifix are both wood, the slab of light under the door that announces Phineas's return to Devon is yellow, the color of Judas and betrayal, and Gene chins himself thirty times the next day in the school's gymnasium.

Yet Christian myth fails to exhaust the tree's meaning. Its rootedness in the earth, its riverbank location, and its overarching branches suggest organic life. Lacking a single meaning, the tree stands for reality itself. Knowles develops this powerful inclusiveness by projecting the tree to several levels of being. For the tree not only exists forcibly at more than one dimension; it also brings together different aspects of reality. Over the spectrum of Gene's life, it is by turns an occasion for danger, friendship, betrayal and regret. Remembered as "a huge lone spike dominating the riverbank, forbidding as an artillery piece," the tree is so much "smaller" and "shrunken by age" fifteen years later that Gene has trouble recognizing it.

Nonetheless, as something more than a physical datum, it marks the turning point of Gene's life and colors the rest of his narrative. The furniture in the home of one of his teachers "shot out menacing twigs," and the tree combines metaphorically with both the War and the aboriginal northern frost to create a strong impression of lostness. The tree's combining power, in fact, is as great as its power to halt or cut short. For while it marks the end of the gipsy summer of 1942, it also yokes Gene's past and present lives.

Friends More Deadly than Enemies

The victim of the tree incident, Phineas, is best summarized by a phrase Knowles uses in *Double Vision* to describe modern Greeks—"a full life lived naturally." . . . Although "an extraordinary athlete . . . the best athlete in the school," Finny stands under five feet nine and weighs only a hundred and fifty pounds. His athletic prowess stems not from brawn but from his superb co-ordination and vitality.

Interestingly, the trophies he wins are for gentlemanly conduct. Finny's mastery goes beyond sports. His great gift is the ability to respond clearly and fully: his "unthinking unity of movement" and his favorite expressions, "naturally" and "perfectly okay," express the harmony and interrelatedness of his life. Finny can afford casualness because he gives himself wholly to his undertakings. There is no room for self-consciousness in this dynamic life-mode. There is no room either for formalized rules. Finny's commitment to life overrides the requirements of reason and law, but not out of innate lawlessness. His responses strike so deeply that, while they sometimes make nonsense of conventional morality, they create their own scale of values.

Finny's organicism also sets the style and tempo of the free, unclassifiable summer of 1942. It must be noted that the separate peace Finny and Gene carve out is no idyllic escape from reality. By founding the Super Suicide Society of the Summer Session, membership in which requires a dangerous leap into the Devon River, the boys admit both danger and death into their golden gipsy days. Accordingly, the game of Blitzball, which Finny invents the same summer, includes the bellicosity and treachery that perhaps count as humanity's worst features: "Since we're all enemies, we can and will turn on each other all the time." Nevertheless, the boys rejoice in Blitzball and, while they sustain a fierce level of competition, they manage to avoid injuries.

For opponents do not inflict pain in the world of *A Separate Peace*; the worst menaces dwell not in rivalry but in friendship. Gene and Phineas become best friends, but Gene cannot live with Finny's goodness. Finny's helping Gene overcome fear and his opening his friend to bracing new adventures rouses Gene's worst traits. Man is a hating rather than a loving animal. . . .

[A] pair of incidents whose variations clarify theme take place in Chapter Three and Chapter Eleven—the third chapter from the end of the novel. The element of Chapter Three is water: Finny breaks Devon's swimming record for the hundred-yard free style, and then swims for an hour in the ocean. By Chapter Eleven the water has frozen.

After walking out of a mock-serious investigation of the tree incident, Finny falls a second time and breaks his leg on the "unusually hard" white marble steps of the First Academy Building. His flowing energy has been immobilized both by Leper's mental breakdown and the loveless efficiency of the investigation. A fact does not count for Finny until he experiences it personally; his head-on encounters with pain and heartlessness kill his belief in universal harmony, and he can no longer deny the ubiquity of war. His separate peace ended, he merges in the last paragraph of Chapter Eleven with the icy discord that gores all of life:

> The excellent exterior acoustics recorded his rushing steps
> and the quick rapping of his cane ... Then these separate
> sounds collide into the general tumult of his body falling
> clumsily down the white marble stairs.

The technique of the last chapter tallies well with both the events and the morality it describes. Knowles violates the unity of time by leaping ahead several months to June 1943; he also breaks a basic rule of fictional art by introducing an important character in his last chapter. These discordancies are intentional: a novel about disjointedness should have its components out of joint with each other. Accordingly, *A Separate Peace* extends a chapter after Phineas's, death and funeral.

But instead of joining its dramatic and thematic climaxes, the last chapter has a scattering effect. Gene's class at Devon has just been graduated, and the boys are shipping out to various branches of the military. The new character, Brinker Hadley's father, is a World War I veteran whose lofty code of patriotism and service means little to the younger generation.

Mr. Hadley cannot, however, be dismissed as a stale anachronism. His argument implies that he knows something the boys have not yet learned. Combat duty is important to him, not as an immediate goal but as a topic to reminisce about in future years. Could Mr. Hadley be suggesting that maturity contains few pleasures and that only a heroic youth can make up for this emptiness? That the boys overlook this implication means little. The chapter is full of communication failures, including the generation rift Mr. Hadley introduces by visiting Devon.

Another new presence at Devon is the U.S. Army. Devon has donated part of its grounds to a Parachute Riggers' school. Appropriately, the sector of the campus used by the soldiers is the Northern Common. But Knowles pulls a shining reversal by overturning this fine narrative stroke. For although the Army as the collective embodiment of man's aggressiveness invades Devon from the icy North, man's aggressiveness has already established a stronghold at Devon. Likewise, the convoy of jeeps driving through campus stirs no warlike fervor. The boyish troops are "not very bellicose-looking," and the jeeps do not contain weapons but sewing machines.

The logic of the novel makes eminent sense of this unlikely freight: the sewing machines, which will service parachutes, allude to the novel's central metaphor of falling, and the young soldiers will lunge headlong into violence in the same way as Devon's Class of 1943. By the end of the book, the malevolence uncoiling from man's fallen nature has engulfed all.

Gene's Peace Is False

Except, strangely, for Gene. His savagery already spent, he has no aggressiveness left for the Navy. Although his country is at war, he is at peace. Yet the armistice is false. A man so askew with his environment enjoys no peace. Gene's lack of purpose not only divides him from his country; it separates him from himself. Divided and subdivided, he is fighting a war just as dangerous as his country's. He has not killed his enemy, as he insists.

His return to Devon in his early thirties and his memoir of Devon's 1942–43 academic year prove that his private struggle has outlasted the public holocaust of World War II. Just as the anvil can break the hammer, the tree incident hurts Gene more than it does Finny. The novel turns on the irony that the separate peace mentioned in its title excludes its most vivid presence—its narrator. Gene's fall 1957 visit to Devon fixes the limits of his fallen life. His self-inventory is either a preparation for life or a statement of withdrawal. But the question of whether he can convert his apartness into a new start goes beyond the boundaries of the novel.

The Duality of War and Peace Is Central to *A Separate Peace*

James M. Mellard

James M. Mellard is professor emeritus of English at Northern Illinois University, where he taught for more than twenty-five years. He is the author of The Exploded Form: The Modernist Novel in America *and the editor of* Style, *"the international journal of aesthetics, poetics, stylistics, and interpretation of film and literature."*

Knowles uses counterpoint in A Separate Peace *to develop his story about the passage from innocence into maturity, suggests Mellard in the following essay. War is contrasted with peace, summer with winter, and the Devon River with the Naguamsett. At the center of the novel is the contrast between the two major characters, Gene and Finny. Just as the other pairs in the novel merge—peace into war, summer into winter, and the Devon River into the Naguamsett—Gene emerges at the end of the novel with some of the characteristics of his friend.*

A Separate Peace, John Knowles's first novel and winner of the first William Faulkner Foundation Award, has become one of the most popular books for literary study in American education since its publication in 1960. The novel is narrated from the point of view of a man looking back over fifteen years at the climactic events of his youth at a New England preparatory school. This retrospective point of view enables Knowles, like [F. Scott] Fitzgerald in *The Great Gatsby*, to present a dual perspective of characters, events, symbols, and settings. Akin, in fact, to the movement of Knowles's recent non-fictional *Double Vision* (1965), the direction of the narrative in the novel is toward the protagonist's recognition

James M. Mellard, "Counterpoint and 'Double Vision' in *A Separate Peace*," *Studies in Short Fiction*, vol. 4, Fall 1966, pp. 127–34. Copyright © 1966 by Studies in Short Fiction. Reproduced by permission.

and acceptance of a puzzling duality, a "double vision," at the very heart of existence. And because of theme and point of view, the demands of symbolism, characterization, and narrative in *A Separate Peace* make counterpoint [a literary technique in which two items are contrasted] the most important technique in Knowles's fiction.

A World at War Mirrors the Battle Within

Arising naturally from setting, the novel's contrapuntal symbolism operates organically in the development of its theme, the growth to maturity through the loss of adolescent innocence and the acceptance of adult experience. The basic symbolism is the contrast between the peace of the school and the war going on outside, for it provides the objective correlative for the subjective battles fought by the youthful characters as they search for personal fulfillment. It is against the war, therefore, that Gene Forrester, the central and point-of-view character of the novel, directs most of his thoughts. To Gene, "The war was and is reality"; and for much of the novel, it is the hard world of reality, of the war, that Gene, at times only unconsciously, hopes to evade, a desire he manages to fulfill, during most of the final school year, through the intervention of his friend Phineas, or "Finny," as he is usually called. Gene says, for example, that "the war swept over like a wave at the seashore, gathering power and size as it bore on us, overwhelming in its rush, seemingly inescapable, and then at the last moment eluded by a word from Phineas . . .". Yet the war, like growth and maturity, can hardly be avoided forever, because "one wave is inevitably followed by another even larger and more powerful, when the tide is coming in." So the youths at Devon, and particularly Gene, enjoy their "momentary, illusory, special and separate peace" whenever they can, just as, during Devon's first Summer Session, the faculty relaxed its controls on the boys because they "reminded them of what peace was like."

Summer Reflects Peace, Winter Reflects War

The fundamental counterpoint between war and peace, reality and illusion, is made more mediate in the symbolic contrast between the "gypsy" summer and the "unromantic" winter. Members of the only summer session in Devon's history, Gene, Phineas and the others make the best of it, managing to break most of the school's rules while still maintaining the faculty's good will, playing at warfare, making up chaotic new games, such as "Blitzball," and forming new clubs, like the "Super Suicide Society of the Summer Session." Supporting the contrast between the reality of the war and the illusions of peace, the opposition between summer and winter is essentially a balancing of the world of fantasy, dream, and desire against the world of fact, even of nightmare and repulsion. As long as the summer lasts, the sense of peace and fulfillment and happiness conquers the encroachments of the war, with its defeats, frustrations and pain: "Bombs in Central Europe were completely unreal to us here, not because we couldn't imagine it ... but because our place here was too fair for us to accept something like that ...". But just as another wave will follow the one eluded, the Winter Session will replace the Summer Session: "It had been the school's first, but this was its one hundred and sixty-third Winter Session, and the forces assembled for it scattered the easygoing summer spirit like so many fallen leaves." At the first Chapel of the new session, Gene thinks how Devon had changed during the summer, how "traditions had been broken, the standards let down, all rules forgotten," but he also realizes that the summer is past, that retribution awaits:

> Ours had been a wayward gypsy music, leading us down all kinds of foolish gypsy ways, unforgiven. I was glad of it, I had almost caught the rhythm of it, the dancing, clicking jangle of it during the summer.

Still it had come to an end, in the last long rays of daylight at the tree, when Phineas fell. It was forced upon me as I sat chilled through the Chapel service, that this probably vindicated the rules of Devon after all, wintery Devon. If you broke the rules, then they broke you. That, I think, was the real point of the sermon on this first morning.

And at this juncture, with school beginning, the summer over, Phineas gone and unlikely to return because of a shattered leg, and the too, too real world of the war reasserting itself, Gene gives himself to the disturbing thought that the "idiosyncratic, leaderless band" of the summer would soon be back under the control of the "official class leaders and politicians." But because the "gypsy days" had intervened and he had absorbed much from Finny, Gene attempts to fight the world alone, a personal battle doomed to failure, but which has momentary triumphs after Finny returns to guide him. The climax of this battle, the "Winter Carnival," is itself a result of the contrast between winter and summer and Gene's desire to restore the spirit of the past summer in the dead of winter. "On this Saturday at Devon," Gene says, "there was going to be no government," and "on this day even the schoolboy egotism of Devon was conjured away." At the Winter Carnival, just before the news of Leper's army desertion, Gene comes closest to regaining the summer place beside his friend Phineas. But this idyllic interlude is followed immediately by Gene's journey through the demonic wintry wasteland of northern New England to see Leper, a trip which reasserts the fact of the war.

Rivers Represent Beauty vs. Ugliness

Another use of counterpoint and one even more specific than the seasonal symbolism is the antithesis between the two rivers that run through the Devon campus and that make the school itself part of the dualistic symbolism. As the summer connotes peace and dream and fantasy, the Devon River represents goodness, beauty, even purity: "going into the Devon

The Phillips Exeter Academy, a boarding school in New Hampshire, was the inspiration for the fictional Devon School in John Knowles's novel A Separate Peace. © Philip Scalia/ Alamy.

was like taking a refreshing shower itself, you never had to clean up after it." It is associated with the cultivated, the pastoral, the idyllic, with the "familiar hills," the "highland farms and forests we knew." The "turbid" Naguamsett, associated with winter, suggests everything contrary to the spirit of the Devon: it is "ugly, saline, fringed with marsh," and it is "governed by unimaginable factors." But as the war overtakes peace, and winter replaces summer, the highland Devon must drop into the lowland Naguamsett, a vicissitude which suggests once again that youth cannot avoid the responsibilities of maturity. So, if the events of the "gypsy summer" take place beside and in the Devon, the events of the winter must take place beside and in the Naguamsett. And where the central image of the summer is Gene and his "best pal" Phineas leaping together into the Devon, in a gesture of brotherhood, the key image of the winter session is Gene and Quackenbush catapulting into the Naguamsett, "in the middle of a fight."

Finny and Gene Are Opposites

In addition to the symbolic counterpoint arising from the temporal and physical settings, contrapuntal character relationships control the development of theme and structure. The major character conflict is that which Gene imagines to exist between him and Finny. Like the novel's symbolism, this conflict grows rather naturally from the setting, for a sense of rivalry often prevails in such schools as Devon. Superficially, it is based upon the school's dual emphasis on athletics and scholarship, because Finny is by far the school's best athlete, while Gene is close to being its very best student. Once Gene decides that they are rivals and that Finny has been artfully concealing his ambitions and attempting to wreck his studies, he decides that they are enemies as well, and, like it or not, they "are even in enmity." But the conflict between Finny and Gene goes much deeper than this, for there are essential oppositions in personality. The fundamental contrast is simply that Gene is all too human and heir to all the weaknesses of flesh and spirit, while Finny, at least as Gene sees him most of the time, is little less than a divinity. Thus where Gene is at times morally and ethically shallow, Finny is the epitome of honesty and openness and fidelity. And yet, of the two, Finny is the nonconformist, for his values are generally self-created, although they never seem self-interested. Thus Gene says,

> . . . I noticed something about Finny's own mind, which was such an opposite from mine. It wasn't completely unleashed after all. I noticed that he did abide by certain rules, which he seemed to cast in the form of commandments. "Never say you are five feet nine when you are five feet eight and a half" was the first one I encountered. Another was, "Always say some prayers at night because it might turn out there is a God."

This last "Commandment" is a good illustration of the quality of Finny's mind, for it in no way represents a self-protective covering of his bets; on the contrary, it shows Finny's desire to see the world as it ought to be; hence Gene's memories are of "Phineas losing even in those games he invented, betting always for what *should* win, for what would have been the most brilliant successes of all, if only the cards hadn't betrayed him." Gene, on the other hand, usually played conservatively, aware at all times of percentages, rules, conventions; consequently, to Gene one of the most astounding of Finny's feats is not so much his breaking a school swimming record without a day of practice, but his unwillingness to have it publicized or even officially recognized, for what Gene values most, at least in the beginning, is conventional and public approval. Thus while Finny has relative values, Gene's values are absolute; where "Finny's life was ruled by inspiration and anarchy," Gene's "was subject to the dictates of [his] own mind, which gave [him] the maneuverability of a strait jacket." And where Finny is the "essence of . . . peace," freedom, courage and selflessness, Gene, until he becomes, as it were, a part of Finny, is swayed by some "ignorance" inside him and trapped by his own guilt and fear and egotism.

Although Knowles insists upon the contrasts between Finny and Gene, he also shows that the two antithetical personalities can, even must, merge into one, just as summer slides into winter, the Devon into the Naguamsett, peace into war. But if these changes seem to be governed by something absolute and unfathomable and yet seem to create something better out of a process that appears undesirable, Gene's transformation also seems to result in a being of greater durability, if not of goodness, one better able to keep his balance in a chaotic world than either the original Gene or Finny. To Gene, Finny is a god, a god of the river, as his name suggests. But, god or man, Finny is not, as Gene tells him, suited for the world as it is, for the war and, thus, for reality. Hence, Phineas, besides his initial contrast to Gene, even points to a strong contrapuntal character symbolism: both the representative of Gene's "fall from innocence" and grace and the means for his deliverance and redemption, in a novel filled with Christian symbols and a theme linked to the concepts of original sin and the fortunate fall, Phineas becomes both Adam and Christ, the "second Adam," in a concentrated, powerful symbolism that is paradoxical, but also traditionally Christian. And, "Phineas-filled" at the novel's conclusion, Gene is enabled to size up the world, like Phineas, "with erratic and entirely personal reservations, letting its rocklike facts sift through and be accepted only a little at a time, only as much as he could assimilate without a sense of chaos and loss."

Counterpoint in Plot and Structure

The uses of counterpoint in symbolism and characterization are important, but they by no means complete *A Separate Peace*. Of equal significance are the contrapuntal devices of plot and structure. There are many actions that have their counteractions in the novel, but the major counterpointed scenes are those that involve Finny's two falls, the markers that determine the three-part structure of the novel. As in symbolism and characterization, the structure of the novel shows a kind of dialectical movement, first revealing the antitheses between the two central figures, then suggesting the "transformation" of one, Gene, into his opposite, and finally portraying, in dramatically convincing ways, the reconciliation of the opposites into one unified, complete and well adjusted personality, who, better than most, can come to terms with the dual attractions of the world.

The climax of part one, at the end of Chapter Four, is the fall of Phineas from the tree beside the Devon River, but it is prepared for by Gene's increasing suspicions and sense of rivalry. Gene's erroneous but nevertheless powerful distrust of Finny begins to emerge when he watches a sunrise at the beach, after Finny had inveigled him to skip school; it culminates when Gene, in a realization that "broke as clearly and bleakly as dawn at the beach," decides that his friend "had deliberately set out to wreck" his studies so that they would not be even. Shortly after, however, at the tree where the "Suicide Society" members test their devotion to the club, Gene recognizes his tremendous spiritual isolation and physical fear, for, although he cannot yet understand why, he realizes that Finny "had never been jealous . . . for a second." So now he realizes more than ever that he "was not of the same quality" as Phineas, a "truth," however, that he cannot abide at all. Moments later, Gene shakes the limb on which they are balancing and causes Finny to fall. The counterpart to this scene of "crime," at the center of which is a ritual test of personal and idiosyncratic values, is the scene of "punishment," the trial that precedes the second fall at the end of Chapter Eleven. The trial reverses the implications of the first fall, for it indicates Gene's progress away from isolation toward social integration.

Just as the scenes preceding the falls are contrasted, the results of the falls are also carefully counterpointed. The major contrast is in the reversal of the influences upon Gene and Phineas: the first fall is far more important to Gene than to Finny, for while it causes physical anguish for Finny, it creates a much greater emotional anguish for Gene. His anguish releases him from fear, but it creates a social guilt and alienation and a corresponding need to identify completely with Phineas, to "become" Phineas, as it were, in order to escape himself. But as Gene grows more and more sure of himself, of his own identity and "real authority and worth," he comes to depend less and less upon Phineas, who was, because of his disability, so dependent upon Gene that he thought of Gene as an "extension of himself." Consequently, the second fall has far greater ramifications for Finny than for Gene. After this accident, Finny is forced to acknowledge the existence of "something blind" in man's character and to accept the fact that Gene caused his original fall because of "some kind of blind impulse." If the ultimate effect of the two falls upon Gene was to make him more capable of existing in the "real" world, their contrary effect upon Finny was simply to destroy him: as Gene had told him long before, Phineas was "too good to be true," so there really could be no place in the world for him, no matter how hard he or Gene might wish it.

Gene Grows into Maturity

Although Phineas is its most memorable character, *A Separate Peace* is Gene's story, and the point of that story is Gene's growing into maturity and accepting his place in the world. Consequently, the most important scene for Gene, after the falls, is his inevitable but painful recognition of the world's and his own duality. This recognition involves the contrast of his youthful, adolescent, "old" way of viewing the world with a more mature, adult, "new" way. Occurring just after Phineas' accident on the stairs, in the building where "boys come to be made men," this scene is the literal and symbolic aftermath of Finny's rejection of Gene. It is actually the climax of the novel because Gene's emotional rejection of Finny's way of life is more important than Finny's death; it shows Gene taking a midnight walk through the campus and sleeping overnight in the stadium. During his walk, Gene says, "I was trying to cope with something that might be called double vision. I saw the gym in the glow of a couple of outside lights near it and I knew of course that it was the Devon gym which I entered every day. It was and it wasn't. There was something innately strange about it, as though there had always been an inner core to the gym which I had never perceived before, quite different from its generally accepted appearance." This "double vision" is true of all else that he sees; everything has a "significance much deeper and far more real than any" he had noticed before, taking on meanings, "levels of reality," he had never suspected. His first impression is that he himself lacked reality, that he was a "ghost," a "dream," a "figment which had never really touched anything." But his real problem as well as his most pressing need are revealed when he says, "I felt that I was not, never had been and never would be a living part of this overpoweringly solid and deeply meaningful world around me."

After the night's sleep in the stadium and the awakening to a fresh new perspective on existence, however, Gene walks back to the "center of the school," has breakfast, gets a notebook from his room and goes to class, actions that suggest powerfully that he has given up Phineas and the stadium, as it were, for his own identity and the classroom. Only now is he enabled again to face Finny with the truth about his first catastrophe and, shortly afterward, to accept, almost without pain, the fact of Finny's death. And it is only after his becoming aware of a double view of reality that Gene steps over the threshold of maturity, now able to recognize existence for what it is, to accept his own position in the world; and to go to war without fear or hatred.

If Phineas has "absorbed" the worst of Gene and taken it with him, Gene has himself absorbed and taken with him the best of Finny—"a way or sizing up the world." Although Gene can "never agree with either" Brinker's or Finny's view of the world ("It would have been comfortable, but I could not believe it."), at least Finny's way of sizing it up with "erratic and entirely personal reservations" allowed one to maintain a coherent, integrated personality. But the key word here is *personal*—one must remain true to himself, his own identity, fulfill his own possibilities rather than another's. So if Gene can never be as innocent as Phineas or regain their "paradise lost," he can at least measure others, as well as himself, against Phineas as he measured the world against Devon, in that prelapsarian [before a fall from grace, a time of innocence] summer of 1942. And if he and the others fall short of Finny's standard, as they must, they will still gain from having reached for it.

War Influences the Peer Relationships in *A Separate Peace*

Hanoch Flum and Harriet Porton

Hanoch Flum is a member of the Department of Education of Ben-Gurion University of the Negev in Israel, and Harriet Porton is a member of the Department of Education of Goucher College.

Using the relationship of Gene and Finny in A Separate Peace *as an example, Flum and Porton in the following essay trace the complexities involved as adolescent males grapple with the formation of their identities. Peer relationships are especially important to adolescents, the authors maintain, and thus teens tend to look for validation in the eyes of their peers.* A Separate Peace *is concerned with the relationship between war and the inner conflicts that cause enmity and violence, according to the authors.*

Adolescents are cognitively capable of thinking about the thoughts of others regarding themselves. Thus, other people, and especially their peers, serve as mirrors. Indeed, a large part of adolescents' relationships are about mirroring as part of the identity formation process. Adolescents tend to explore themselves by gazing at real mirrors, and they learn about themselves by looking at their image in the eyes of others. At the same time, they become aware of subjective elements of knowledge and tend to cast doubt and to question. Adolescents' questioning and entertaining possibilities are primarily directed toward the self, and the differences in intensity

Hanoch Flum and Harriet Porton, "Relational Processes and Identity Formation in Adolescence: The Example of *A Separate Peace*," *Genetic, Social & General Psychology Monographs*, vol. 121, November 1995, pp. 369–90. Reprinted by permission of the publisher (Taylor & Francis Ltd., http://www.informaworld.com) and the authors.

of such explorations can reflect the differentiation in styles of identity formation. . . .

At a time of developmental transition, and certainly in adolescence, the individual who is engaged in restructuring the self is tuned to the questions, What does the other know about me? and Can the other feel and understand what is inside me? Yet to untangle some of the internal confusion and to feel validated, the adolescent needs the other. And the "other" who is expected to be closest understanding and to mirror most directly is a peer. Adolescent peers understand, identify, reflect, support, and judge.

The judgments that adolescents pass on their peers can be merciless. "Never are people more unforgiving mirrors for each other than in youth. . . . The developing person learns about his or her worth, who he or she is, in others' eyes" [writes R. Josselson in *The Space Between Us: Exploring the Dimensions of Human Relationships*]. But the process of finding oneself in another is shifting and multileveled rather than discrete and unidirectional. The subtleties of the process are well portrayed in *A Separate Peace*.

Setting the Stage

In our interpretation of the relationships between adolescents in John Knowles's *A Separate Peace*, our focus is on Gene, the person who tells the story, but what unfolds is the larger narrative of the identity formation of adolescent boys.

The context of the story is World War II. The war is always in the background and is reflected in the story on a number of levels, from the internal to the external. The book describes the atmosphere at the somewhat isolated Devon School in New Hampshire, USA. The war's presence is felt through reports from the frontline, recruiters who visit the school, and the juniors and seniors who wrestle with the question of whether to enlist. War influences the games that are played and the boys' views of themselves and their peers. War is echoed in the boys' relationships, fears, and internal struggles.

The novel's background theme of war and peace heightens the elements of interest to us: the relational battlefield and the war as part of reality, a reflection of the confusion of the outside adult world. At the same time, from another perspective, *A Separate Peace* is a story of closeness and love and the effort to find oneself. In narrating the evolving friendship of Gene and Phineas, Knowles tells a tale of love and identity that cycles through rivalry, envy, and enmity. . . .

The story of Gene and Finny revolves around the experience of the power of the idealized self-object and Gene's effort to wrestle with it and to make' peace with it. The process goes through curves and spins, but the movement in Gene's development is toward learning about himself, overcoming "false identity," and mastering his "own real authority and worth."

Adolescents' preoccupation with "what they appear to be in the eyes of others compared with what they feel they are" was pointed out by [E.M. Erikson in *Identity: Youth and Crisis*]. Erikson referred to the mirroring process in conjunction with idealizations in adolescence, which are also linked to cultural icons, to what is valued and lauded in the larger society. What is aspired to is what others admire.

Among American adolescent boys nothing can compete with the status of sports. Being a good athlete is highly valued and can earn admiration among peers. And Finny is an outstanding athlete, winning many prizes as an individual and in team games. It earns him a leadership position in his peer group, and it inspires Gene's admiration. Thus, when Finny notices that the school record in free-style swimming hasn't been broken since they have been at school, he immediately feels challenged to break it. He switches to a new sport that he hasn't competed in before, and he breaks the record. "There was something inebriating in the suppleness of this feat," Gene reports. "It had, in one word, glamour, absolute school- boy glamour." Gene's experience is one of "shock;" a shock deepened by Finny's insistence that his great achievement, which no one else has witnessed, must remain a secret be- tween them. "It made Finny too unusual for—not friendship, but too unusual for rivalry."

When a challenge comes from Finny to break all the rules by biking to the beach because "real swimming is in the ocean," Gene can't refuse. He goes along, even though he has a number of reasons not to, including an important test the next morning. The bike trip is an opportunity not only for tricks and amusement but for mirroring as well: "[Finny] ana- lyzed my character, and he insisted on knowing what I dis- liked most about him."

Adolescents' preoccupation with how they are perceived by the other is well reflected here. The mirroring process is work- ing both ways. We have already argued that the combination of mirroring and idealization is powerful, illustrated by Gene's evidence. However, the process becomes more complicated when Gene becomes aware that Phineas, in turn, idealizes him. . . .

Finny's feelings are unequivocal and direct. Nevertheless, Gene, idealizing Finny, still cannot accept being on an equal footing with Finny in any way. It is confusing to find out that the idol whom you worship idealizes you. Indeed, Gene be- comes clearly aware that Phineas idealizes him, when he later finds that Phineas, who thinks that Gene doesn't need to study to succeed, "made some kind of parallel between my studies and his sports. . . . He didn't know yet that he was unique." At that point in the story, that awareness is not spelled out. But it is hinted at; it is an undercurrent that eventually contributes to a whirlpool of confusion. . . .

Relationship and Identity

Adolescents need each other to grow. The complexity of their relationships may obscure some of the most important dimensions in which they relate to each other, the processes that are fundamental to their identity formation and tend to be overlooked by research. Gene's narrative tells the relational story of Gene and Phineas. In the present article we have traced the shifts and transformations in their connection as they reflect on their identity formation.

Adolescents tend to be preoccupied with how they are "seen" by others. In their attempt to define their identity they look at their reflection in the other and gradually clarify their self-image.... Moreover, as clearly illustrated in the story we have followed and analyzed, identity formation is not a linear developmental process. It involves progression and regression, confusion and clarification (and more confusion and clarification), interpretations and construction.

Early in the story two pals realize their friendship. Gene feels validated by Phineas, who is emphatic and challenging. Finny, who is developed into an idealized self-object, is a very strong influence on Gene. A highly admired mirror can be very effective, and Gene feels valued. Their relationship shifts when it becomes clearer that the idealization works both ways; Gene begins to feel too transparent, senses his need for separation, and starts to question the motives of the idealized other as a result of his failure. At that point, mirroring, which requires a basis of trust and value, is to a large extent deactivated. Finny is defined as an enemy in Gene's newly constructed world. The rivalry and envy, as well as the need to contrast and compete with Finny, feed Gene's identity and motivate him to succeed academically.

After the deidealization, a collapse of the assumption on which Gene's world was temporarily constructed, and then the resumption of a certain idealization and revival of the self-object, Gene experiences much confusion. Who is he? How could he misinterpret Finny's motives? From where does it come in him? Confusion in adolescence can lead to exploration and, eventually, to resolution. But the confusion can also become overwhelming, resulting in radical attempts to free the self from its burden.

The boys' effort to bond again fails with Finny's injury. Guilt adds to the confusion, driving Gene's search for identity into an attempt at total identification with Finny, at becoming Finny. Adopting a false self and entering a twinship relationship mark another phase in the relationship as well as in Gene's identity formation. Enclosed in a private world, merging, they live in a fantasy invented by Phineas and adopted by Gene, who would do anything to please Finny. They invest themselves in each other, defending their illusory world.

Adolescents tend to look for a cause, and they sometimes create a fantasy that directs their energy and sustains their relationships. In fantasy, they may defend themselves from reality's demands. The case of Gene and Phineas is an extreme one (fed by the context of war, the isolated school, Phineas's injury and Gene's guilt, along with other factors). They shut themselves off from the confusion of war, the reality of the outside world, and the necessity of growing up.

Gene's identity during this phase is determined by Finny's expectations and by Gene's wish to fulfill them. He is assigned the identity of the athlete who is training for the Olympic Games. For a while, he gains peace and happiness in that role.

The calm is shattered by Leper in the trial, when he offers a window on reality to the classmates in pursuit of the "truth." They serve as [what Josselson in *The Space Between Us* calls] "unforgiving mirrors" who judge harshly, triggering a process that leads to a separation, Finny's death, and Gene's rebirth.

A *Separate Peace* Depicts Male Bonding

Eric L. Tribunella

Eric L. Tribunella is an assistant professor of English at the University of Southern Mississippi, where he teaches children's and young adult literature. He is the author of Melancholia and Maturation: The Use of Trauma in American Children's Literature.

In the following article, considered groundbreaking because it was one of the first to claim a homosexual attachment between Gene and Finny, Tribunella charts Gene's growth to manhood in A Separate Peace. *Initially attracted to Finny, over the course of the novel Gene grows into adulthood and heterosexuality. Participating in war has homoerotic implications for young men, the author claims, because it is socially acceptable in wartime for young men to forge deep attachments and to mourn when comrades die.*

[*A Separate Peace*] is framed by the narration of Gene, who returns to Devon School fifteen years later to reminisce about his coming of age. By beginning and concluding the novel with the insights of an adult Gene, Knowles preestablishes the inevitable culmination of the story's movement—Gene as a man. The reader is allowed to glimpse who Gene will become, and the story told as a flashback provides the map of the course Gene follows. Hence, the process of gendering the boy to "be a man" lies at the heart of *A Separate Peace*, and the conflicts and actions it details serve to further this process as its central project.

Eric L. Tribunella, "Refusing the Queer Potential: John Knowles's *A Separate Peace*," *Children's Literature*, vol. 30, 2002, pp. 81–96. Copyright © 2002 by The Johns Hopkins University Press. Reproduced by permission.

Gene Refuses to Admit His Feelings for Finny

Finny's and Gene's relationship is characterized by a subtle homoeroticism in which Gene eroticizes Finny's innocence, purity, and skill, and Finny eroticizes the companionship provided by Gene. With World War II serving throughout the novel as the backdrop against which the "peace" of Devon is contrasted, the boys initially engage in the ritual of taking off their clothes and jumping from a tall tree into the river below as practice for the possibility of having to jump from a sinking ship in battle. Jumping from the tree acquires special significance for Finny and Gene; it serves as a sign of loyalty and as an act that cements their bond and stands in for sexual play. . . .

Finny demonstrates his interest in sharing intimate moments with Gene when he encourages him to skip class and spend a day at the beach. Finny reveals in his characteristically honest way that Gene is the "proper" person with whom to share such moments as they settle down to sleep on the sand. Gene considers such a naked emotional expression to be next to suicide at Devon, and he remains unable to reciprocate Finny's admission. Gene does, however, notice Finny's physical attractiveness even if he must project this sentiment onto the anonymous passersby: "I noticed that people were looking fixedly at him, so I took a look myself to see why. His skin radiated a reddish copper glow of tan, his brown hair had been a little bleached by the sun, and I noticed that the tan made his eyes shine with a cool bluegreen fire." Gene notices Finny's appearance, though Finny is the first to say about Gene, "Everybody's staring at you. It's because of that movie star tan you picked up this afternoon . . . showing off again." While Gene reciprocates Finny's feelings, he cannot bring himself to admit them as Finny does. Gene's self-preserving silence allows him to resist both the possibility and the threat of consummating his platonic friendship with Finny, whereas Finny's willingness to expose his emotional vulnerabilities predicts his eventual expulsion from a context that forbids such expressions.

Gene's Homosexual Panic

Gene allays the confusions that result from his affection for Finny and the tumult of emotions such forbidden feelings arouse in him by first causing the accident that forces Finny's disappearance from Devon and then incorporating Finny into himself. Following their trip to the beach, the night they spend alone there, and Finny's intimate expression of his fondness for Gene, Gene finds himself growing increasingly suspicious of Finny and attributes this reaction to the possibility that Finny plans to sabotage his grades. Finny and Gene later return to the tree where, after undressing, Finny suggests that they jump together hand-in-hand, an act that could substitute for a strictly forbidden sexual act between the boys. They climb the tree and prepare to jump, but in a moment of panic, Gene jounces the limb and sends Finny crashing to the ground, thereby setting a series of events in motion that culminates in Finny's death. His realization that Finny's intentions are not dishonest after all, coupled with Finny's suggestion that they take the jump together, ignites the moment of homosexual panic. Gene responds to Finny's advances with an act of violent separation. Finny's attempt to take Gene's hand triggers the need in Gene to conform to the heterosexual imperative that forecloses the possibility of same-sex desire by forcibly detaching himself from Finny. . . .

Following Finny's first departure from Devon School and Gene's incorporation of the loss as an identification within his own ego, Gene determines along with Brinker to enlist in the war effort and, in doing so, the masculine environs of the military and battlefield. The war propels the boys forward, away from their adolescent shelter and toward the final phase of their initiation into manhood. The return of Finny fore-

A still from the 1972 film adaptation of the novel A Separate Peace. *Parker Stevenson and John Heyl play Gene and Finny, respectively.* © Paramount Pictures Corporation.

stalls Gene's entrance into the war, and the reemergence of the queer possibility effectively suspends Gene's enlistment and the verification of his masculinity. The threat posed by Finny becomes evident. His presence, in fact, his continued existence, defers indefinitely Gene's "ascension" to a proper manhood. Finny must therefore die to prevent any further return and to allow Gene to claim finally his masculinity and complete the gendering process that is ongoing throughout *A Separate Peace*.

Grief and Love During Wartime

Mark Simpson has described [in "Don't Die on Me, Buddy: Homoeroticism and Masochism in War Movies"] the buddy war film as a compilation of lessons about masculinity and how to take one's place in patriarchy. Simpson's analysis of such films can be used to examine Knowles's novel, since the lingering war provides the context for Finny's and Gene's homoerotic friendship. Simpson describes the intimate relationship between same-sex desire and death established in the war film as the necessary condition for any expression of homodesire:

> In war films of the buddy type the deadliness of war is not glossed over. But it is portrayed not in the death of the enemy, who are often faceless or even unseen, but in the death of the comrades and buddies. Classically, the moment when the buddy lies dead or dying is the moment when the full force of the love the boys/men feel for one another can be shown. And, for all the efforts of the conscientious film maker, the deadliness is thus attached not as much to war as to the queer romance of it all. . . .

Gene's participation in the war effort is fueled by this disavowed loss of the homosexual attachment, and if Gene's development is taken to represent a collectively experienced process by which boys are made men, then it might be said that the war itself is predicated on the ungrieved loss of homosexual attachment. On the battlefield, men can place themselves in positions to be killed by the enemy such that death comes from without, and mourning one's comrades in war can stand in for mourning the homosexual attachment that was lost. The trauma of war as a purely masculine pursuit serves as a pretext for the grief that cannot be experienced at home during peacetime. One can love one's comrades and grieve their loss with the displaced love and loss "never" felt for the original same-sex object. Any resistance to the imperative that demands such an oppressive masculinity formed on the disavowal of homo-desire can be directed towards the enemy, and any guilt suffered over one's own compliance can be transformed into a hatred of this enemy. War might be described as the only appropriate place for experiencing this grief, and the possibility of eliminating this motivation for war (as it certainly is not the only motivation) presents a useful rationale for refusing the loss of homosexual attachment and for changing the conditions that initially demand its loss.

The context of Devon School during wartime conflates the school and the battlefield. Seeking to act out the war, Finny invents the game of Blitzball in which the boy with the ball must run from one side of the field to the other without being tackled. At any point in the game, the player holding the ball could pass it on to another player who would then become the object of attack for the other boys. One must pass the ball according to Finny, who invents a game with no teams. Each player is simultaneously an adversary and an ally, so these terms effectively have no meaning in the context of Blitzball in which players fluidly shift between roles never fixed in relation to other players. One can never identify allies or enemies in Blitzball, making it a queer game resisting the fixity of identities. Rather than enforcing the strict dichotomization of sides, Finny rejects this fundamental attribute of competition, thereby creating a space from which to expose it as not inevitable. Finny also adopts this resistant tactic during a snowball fight when he again begins switching sides so that "loyalties became hopelessly entangled." A classmate follows suit, leading Gene to describe him as a eunuch.

Finny repeatedly produces the central symbols of the novel. He initiates the practice of jumping from the tree, a practice that acquires significance as a site for both the sealing of Finny's friendship with Gene and their separation. During Finny's temporary return to Devon following his injury he begins training Gene for the Olympics in which he himself had wished to participate. Despite the impossibility of such a goal, Finny's encouragement persists in maintaining it as a realistic possibility in their minds, again demonstrating his authority over the boys' fantasies. Finny also determines the symbolic value of the pink shirt, which he dons as an emblem ostensibly to demonstrate his pride in the Allied victories over Central Europe. Gene expresses concern that Finny's pink shirt might cause others to "mistake" him for a "fairy," a concern to which Finny responds "mildly . . . I wonder what would happen if I looked like a fairy to everyone." Finny's lack of concern is itself queer in the homosocial context of a boys' school where, by the 1940s, such a label might incur a significant cost to one's social status, if not physical safety. The pink shirt, moreover, proves central to Gene's attempt to become Finny. Wearing the shirt completes Gene's incorporation of Finny into his own self following Finny's first absence from Devon. That Finny originates each of these symbols signifies a phallic authority ultimately claimed by Gene as the story's narrator.

Leper as Failure to Confront Homoeroticism

In contrast to Gene, his schoolmate Leper fails to undergo the same process by which Gene achieves manhood. Leper is—as one might predict from his name—an outsider, never fully participating in the boys' society, never playing their games, preferring instead to wander alone in the woods. He finally leaves Devon to enlist, "escapes" from the army, and returns to school to testify in Gene's mock trial. In this allegory of gender construction, Leper represents the boy who neither refuses the loss of homosexual attachment nor consummates a potential union. He therefore never incorporates the possible object of desire within his ego, thereby proving malformed and dysfunctional as a result of his failure to adhere to the normative developmental trajectory followed by Gene. When Finny first jumps from the tree Leper refuses to join in the ritual with the other boys. In response to Finny's insistence on Leper's participation, Gene recalls that "Leper closed his mouth as though forever. He didn't argue or refuse. He didn't back away. He became inanimate." Leper simply watches and so bears witness to the symbolic attachment created as an unrealized possibility between Finny and Gene. At the crucial moment when Gene jounces the limb and sends Finny crashing to the ground in a violent moment of homosexual panic—the refusal of the queer possibility—Leper stands by as the only witness to the event, silently observing the mechanisms by which Gene undertakes to assume his masculinity and authorized position in patriarchy. Although the other boys work clearing snow from the railroad yard to permit trains carrying new military recruits to pass, Leper abstains from this contribution to the war effort, choosing instead to keep his distance and explore the forest trails. Ultimately Leper enlists in the army only to suffer a mental breakdown and go "psycho."

At the climax of the novel when the boys try Gene for maiming Finny, Leper arrives to present the damning evidence, his testimony that Gene deliberately caused Finny's accident. Faced with this evidence, Finny flees from the truth and finally dies at the end of the sequence of events put in motion by Gene. In the context of the trial, Leper occupies the place of the critic, the one who reads through the allegory and exposes the underlying mechanisms motivating Gene's violent act. Leper stands as a figure that warns the reader to avoid reading too closely or looking too intently to uncover the reason for Gene's violence. The processes of achieving heterosexuality and masculinity cannot be completed properly in the witness if he becomes too aware of their workings. The figure of Leper functions in the story to present the potential risk of insanity to the student who might be drawn to the position of the critic. The student should not be a witness who observes directly these mechanisms of gender construction since insanity looms as a possible punishment. . . .

The lingering question still posed by students, however, is "Why must Finny die?". If the question is motivated by a desire to see Finny live, then it marks a potential impetus for the student to produce a resistant reading of the text. The question, "Why does Finny have to die?" could represent the student's desire to see the homosexual attachment completed, or at least not entirely foreclosed before the possibility of con-

summation is realized. Finny must die precisely because he refuses to reject the possibility of loving Gene.

Contemporary Perspectives on War

The War on Terror Is Causing Bullying of Sikh Teens

Julianne Ong Hing

Julianne Ong Hing is an editorial assistant at Colorlines *magazine.*

The war on terror is causing a backlash of school bullying aimed at children of Muslim, Arabic, and Sikh ancestry, reports Hing in the following viewpoint. Although Sikhs are a religious group originally from India and are neither Muslim nor Arabic, because of their appearance and the turbans males wear, they have become targets of anti-Muslim racial bullying. More than 65 percent of Sikh students in Queens, New York, report that they have been physically or verbally abused, according to a 2007 report cited by the author. High school can be a difficult time for most adolescents, Hing states, and racial intimidation makes it worse.

Adjusting to high school always takes time, especially when you're the new kid on the block. But for Jagmohan Singh Premi, a practicing Sikh with quiet, almond-shaped eyes, school only became scarier and more dangerous the more time he spent there. The teenager endured daily epithets— "terrorist" and "bin Laden" were most common—and taunts about his turban and beard during his freshman year at Richmond Hill High School in Flushing, Queens. He had just emigrated to the United States from India the year before.

Sikhs Find Racism at School and Work

As required by his faith, Premi kept his uncut hair bundled in a small turban, called a patka, which students would tear off his head. Despite repeated appeals by Premi to school administrators for intervention, the main perpetrator continued to torment him. Last June (2009), the perpetrator not only tried to pull Premi's patka off but also punched Premi in the eye with keys gripped between his knuckles in the middle of class. Premi suffered a swollen and bloodied eye.

When Sikh community advocates demanded to speak with administrators, they were met with indifference.

"The assistant principal didn't get that pulling off his turban would be a violation of his Sikh identity," said Sonny Singh, an organizer with the Sikh Coalition, a national advocacy group. "It wasn't until someone said that would be the equivalent of attempting to remove a Jewish boy's yarmulke that she got it."

Premi's family didn't face racism only on school grounds. His father worked for National Wholesale Liquidators, a New York company recently found guilty of religious and sexual harassment of its Sikh employees. The company has since filed for bankruptcy, and Premi's father has lost his job. "If it's not the father facing it, it's the child," said Amardeep Singh, executive director of the Sikh Coalition.

The physical assault [in] June was the last straw for Premi, whose family pulled him out of the school, but it was no surprise for the Sikh community in the Richmond Hill community in Flushing, where the majority of Sikh students report being targeted for racial bullying at school. In 2008, a spate of incidents aimed at Sikh students across the city made headlines after they turned violent.

Sixty-five percent of Sikh students in Queens, New York, experience some kind of racial intimidation or bullying, ranging from verbal assaults to physical violence, according to a study released by the Sikh Coalition in 2007. Others though think the rates are even higher.

"I would venture to say the real number is close to a hundred percent," said Steve Wessler, the executive director of the Center for the Prevention of Hate Violence, a group that develops curriculum and conducts trainings to combat prejudice. Wessler added that his group has seen racial harassment increasingly turn into hate crimes in schools over the last decade because enduring racist attitudes are being compounded by anti-immigrant and anti-Muslim bias in the country. "When it seems no one else takes it seriously, it becomes normalized," he said. "Being called a terrorist becomes background noise."

Sonny Singh pointed to pervasive racism and xenophobia [fear of those who are different from oneself], encouraged by U.S. policies of detention and deportation and the War on Terror abroad, as the fuel for the racial bullying in schools. "Over the summer, when Barack Obama was called Muslim, John McCain said, 'No, he's not an Arab. He's a good man,'" recalled Singh. "Islamaphobia [fear of Islams] is spiraling out of control."

Sikhs, a religious group originally from Punjab, India, whose communities number 30,000 in Richmond Hill and 25,000 in New Jersey, have been caught in the crossfire of hate along with Muslims and Arabs. "With Sikhs in particular, we have been racially constructed by mainstream society as Arabs or Muslims," said Sonny Singh, adding that violence against any community is deplorable.

"If you think of it as interlocking, overlapping Olympic rings, Sikh kids are viewed as immigrants whether they are or not. They are viewed as Muslim or Arab and viewed as terrorists. And they're kids of color," said Wessler. "When you put all of those together, it is much, much more than the sum of its parts."

Premi's family transferred him to a new school, where he has the support of teachers and administrators who have been attentive to his needs as a new immigrant struggling with English. His parents have since filed a lawsuit against Richmond Hill High School for violating his civil rights and allowing his daily harassment.

For many in the Sikh community, Premi's story reminded them of what happened in 2007 when 15-year-old Harpal Vacher had his hair cut by a classmate and flushed down the toilet at his Queens high school. And in May of 2008, when Garrett Green set a Sikh schoolmate's patka on fire during a fire drill at Hightstown High School in New Jersey. When, five days after Premi's attack 12-year-old Gurprit Kaur had her hair cut off and thrown in the trash by a classmate at PS 219 in Flushing, the community was sparked to protest.

Kaur's brother Talwinder Singh was often called a "potato head" and a "turbanator." Classmates would yell that his patka was a bomb and that people should run away from him because he was going to blow up everyone around him. "I like school," said Talwinder Singh, "but not the kids."

Instruction in Hate-Crime Prevention Needed

In July 2008, 200 people marched from two Sikh temples in Flushing to the Richmond Hill High School to demand that the Department of Education take action to end the racial bullying so rampant in New York City schools. "We have no elected officials, no votes. All we have is public embarrassment or lawsuits," said Amardeep Singh.

By the end of the summer, more than 1,800 signatures were gathered from people demanding transparency, reporting and action from the Department of Education. The agitation and public shaming worked. In September, Mayor Bloomberg and New York Chancellor of Schools Joel Klein announced a resolution to regulate the reporting and response to racial bullying in schools.

According to Sonny Singh, the new regulation will establish a protocol for school officials to track and investigate bias-based bullying on their campuses. Administrators are required to report every incident of bias-based bullying, designate a point person who kids can report incidents to and institute training on anti-bias initiatives.

But Sonny Singh is hesitant to say that the resolution alone will solve the problems plaguing Sikh kids. "The way the resolution is written right now, a principal could invite his brother or sister to do a training and then check that box off," Singh said.

Better reporting of incidents, while popular as a policy point, won't be enough to change the culture of schools and the institutionalized racism that undergirds these schoolyard hate crimes.

Wessler suggests that schools like Richmond Hill High School can affect change by having adults trained in hate crime prevention sit down with students and facilitate face-to-face dialogue for several weeks. "We have seen dramatic evidence that yes, in fact, when people start communication directly, prejudice goes down," Wessler said. "Until you empower kids to stand up for other kids across racial, ethnic and religious lines, there's only so much that administrators can do."

The Teenagers of Afghanistan Attend School Amid the Hardships of War

James Palmer

James Palmer is a reporter and photographer who has covered stories in the Middle East and Africa.

Children in war-torn Afghanistan are struggling against odds to attend school and enjoy the pleasures of childhood despite the turmoil that surrounds them, Palmer reports in the following article. Under the rule of the Taliban, girls were forbidden to attend school. With the Taliban ousted from power following the U.S. invasion of Afghanistan after the 9/11 attacks, about 2 million Afghan girls are now going to school; however, the insurgent Islamic militants are making it difficult for many students to do so. More than six hundred schools were closed in 2008, and female students and teachers have been the targets of violence by the Taliban insurgents.

Marizia Shatob, 13, walks to school each day with a white scarf around her head and a book bag slung over her shoulder. Her classroom, which is located in Kabul, Afghanistan's capital, is barely furnished. In it, you will find dilapidated wooden desks and a battered chalkboard. There, Marizia and more than two dozen other girls study math, science, history, and literature.

Until recently, such a scene was unimaginable in Afghanistan. From 1996 to 2001, this nation of nearly 33 million people was ruled by the Taliban, a fundamentalist Islamic group that prohibited education among girls.

Then came September 11, 2001, when Al Qaeda terrorists launched deadly attacks on the United States. Afghanistan refused to turn over Al Qaeda leader Osama bin Laden, who was thought to be hiding in the country. As a result, U.S.-led forces invaded Afghanistan and toppled the Taliban.

The U.S. helped to install an elected government, led by President Hamid Karzai. After decades of war against Soviet and Taliban forces, Afghans began to rebuild their country and enjoy more freedoms. Today, Marizia is one of about 2 million Afghan girls who are at last able to attend school.

Limits to Schooling

But Afghanistan's troubles are far from over. The Taliban has been battling back and now controls much of the country. The 32,000 U.S. troops stationed in Afghanistan, along with 50,000 others from an international coalition, struggle to contain them.

In the fighting, the Taliban have managed to erase some of the progress achieved in Afghans' education. More than 600 schools have been forced to close, say officials. This prevented about 300,000 students from attending school last year [2008].

Islamic militants have also burned down schools, thrown acid on girls' faces, and murdered female students and teachers.

Despite these threats, Marizia is determined to continue her education. "I want to attend university one day and study medicine," she tells JS [*Junior Scholastic*]. "These attacks will not stop me from going to school."

Marizia says that most Afghans oppose the Taliban and their extreme interpretation of Islam. "They don't practice Islam," she says. "Banning girls from going to school is not Islamic. They just want to destroy the country."

Marzim Nikzad, 12, is a seventh-grader at the Satara Public School in the Shashdark neighborhood of northern Kabul. She too has a negative view of the Taliban. "The Taliban don't

Afghan boys arriving at school. Amid the hardships of war, Afghan children struggle to attend school. AP Images.

want girls to study and receive an education," she says. "They want girls to be illiterate and shut in the house."

More U.S. Troops?

Last year [2008] was Afghanistan's most violent since 2001. According to one United Nations estimate, 1,145 Afghan civilians were killed in the first eight months. These included 52 children who died when rebels attacked a school. U.S. bombs killed 60 more children during one August battle with insurgents (rebels). In all, about 395 of these civilian deaths came from U.S. and international coalition air strikes.

The year 2008 was also the deadliest for coalition troops there, with an estimated 294 killed in combat. Most of the fighting took place along Afghanistan's southeastern border with Pakistan. U.S. drones have fired rockets aimed at militants on both sides of the border. Pakistan's government objects to attacks on its soil. But U.S. officials say that the strikes are necessary because Al Qaeda and bin Laden are using the area as a sanctuary.

U.S. President Barack Obama has pledged to send up to 30,000 more U.S. troops to Afghanistan. Critics argue, however, that the U.S. is in danger of getting enmeshed in an endless war in the country's forbidding mountains. They also warn that militants driven from Afghanistan will just go to nuclear-armed Pakistan, further endangering that country's fragile peace.

Obama's pledge has sparked debate among Afghans about the place of the U.S. military in their country. "I'm not happy they're here, because Afghanistan belongs to the Afghan people," says Marizia. "They came to bring peace, but they've killed many civilians."

Sayeed Ahmed Zaki, 14, is in the ninth grade at the Habibia School in south Kabul. He believes that Obama's plan will work. "I'm optimistic Obama will bring peace to the country with his promise of more U.S. troops," he tells JS. "The insurgents are targeting and killing civilians in suicide bombings. The U.S. troops are not targeting civilians."

Hard Times

Afghanistan is a poor, largely rural country. Illiteracy, particularly among women and girls, remains high. More than two thirds of Afghans over age 15 cannot read or write.

Outside of Kabul, few areas have electricity and many lack clean water. The capital also has its share of problems. Sayeed's family receives only five hours of electrical power once every three days. Unemployment is high, and crime in the city has risen. The streets are filled with women, children, and older men begging for a living. Many of them are among the 5 million refugees who have returned to Afghanistan in recent years.

Adding to these hardships, a severe drought has destroyed crops and livestock across large parts of the country. Near one quarter of Afghans face food shortages this winter.

The country's most profitable crop is the poppy, which is used to produce most of the world's supply of the drugs opium and heroin. Corrupt government officials, the Taliban, and local warlords all benefit from the illegal drug trade.

Afghans generally support President Karzai because he is viewed as an honest leader. "But he doesn't have enough support from others in government," says Sayeed's classmate Waris Ahmed Faizi, 14. "There are too many corrupt officials. Karzai can't improve the country alone."

Everywhere, Afghan parents worry about their children's safety and their ability to get a good education. "My great hope is that my son will have the opportunity to study outside of Afghanistan one day," says Nazir Mohammed, Waris's father.

A Special Sport

Despite the obstacles, daily life in Afghanistan remains lively. Kids in Kabul shoot marbles on the streets. They play soccer on dirt fields and volleyball in dusty lots, and keep flocks of birds as pets.

Students go to school from Saturday to Thursday. Fridays are a holiday, in observance of the Muslim day of prayer. On that day, many Afghans cast their kites skyward. Kite fighters battle with sharp wires or string coated with ground glass, trying to cut their opponent's line and send that kite fluttering away.

"Kite fighting is a special sport in Afghanistan," 12-year-old Saeed Adris tells JS. The Taliban once banned the pastime, but it is again widely practiced.

Saeed's father, Khaila Adris, owns a kite shop in Kabul. Kite fighting survived the Taliban, he says, and he predicts it will outlast the country's current crisis.

"The situation here is bad now," Adris says. "But many people are still buying and flying kites."

Young Iraqis Value Security and Jobs over Democracy

Jane Arraf

Jane Arraf is a correspondent for the Christian Science Monitor.

Teenagers in Iraq, tired of a war that has gone on for most of their lives, long for peace. When asked about the election to be held in March 2010, most young Iraqis say democracy takes a backseat to coping with the challenges of daily life, Arraf reports in the following article. While the opportunity to participate in a democratic election should be exciting to young people, many young Iraqis are frustrated with the lack of jobs and security and doubt that government can do anything to help them.

R adio host Shahad Abdul Kareem, the rhinestones on her T-shirt and sequined headband sparkling, sits in the semi-darkness of the Voice of Fallujah studio waiting for the generator to kick in so she can reach out to young listeners and find out what's on their minds.

Young Iraqis Remember the Saddam Era as Safe

In the run-up to the most important parliamentary elections since the fall of [Iraqi dictator] Saddam Hussein, members of this generation of first-time voters are not so much preoccupied with politics as with the difficulties of day-to-day life. Day after day, they pour out their miseries over Fallujah's airwaves.

"The first thing they mention is frustration," says Ms. Abdul Kareem, 25, whose name is an on-air pseudonym. The frustration stems from lack of jobs and lack of security. The second is the financial situation. One recent caller was a 32-year-old engineer who couldn't get married. Another was a young woman who hadn't been able to bathe for a week because there was never enough electricity to heat the water for everyone in the house.

"For us as Iraqi youth, we haven't seen anything nice in our life," says Abdul Kareem, who describes seeing shrapnel fly through her home before the battle for Fallujah.

Fallujah, west of Baghdad, was leveled in 2004 when US and Iraqi troops went into Al Qaeda strongholds. For the US, it was the fiercest urban fighting since the Vietnam War. For families, and teachers, and shopkeepers and their children, it was a nightmare. Whether disaffected Sunnis [one of two major Muslim sects] like those in Fallujah turn out to vote in March [2010] is key to the election's credibility and, eventually, to whether the country will hold together.

"I don't want to be too ambitious because I'm afraid that, if my ambitions don't turn out, I will be hugely disappointed," says Abdul Kareem.

Asked what she would dream of if she dared to, her guarded manner slips for a moment. "Many things," she says with a broad smile. "I wish I could continue my studies and get a degree, I wish I could travel. I wish it was like it was before, when I could go out with my friends and feel safe."

"Before" was the 1990s—the Saddam era, a time that many remember as almost idyllic in its safety. Unless their own families were victims of Saddam's terror, in between the 1991 war and the 2003 invasion, the streets of Iraq held almost no threats. Young women could go out to visit their friends in the evening, families dined at outdoor restaurants until after midnight, parks were full, life seemed less precarious.

In many ways, what young Iraqis want from their leaders mirrors what any Iraqi adult wants—electricity, water, security, and jobs. Those were the most basic of expectations set up after the fall of Saddam and, seven years later, they remain largely unfulfilled. For most, democracy runs far behind.

"What did we gain from the first elections?" asks Ali Khutiar Abbas, at 19 already a father of three living in Baghdad's predominantly Shiite [the other major Muslim sect] Sadr City. "We don't have jobs, we haven't seen any change in the security situation. I won't vote for anyone—I don't believe in elections anymore. This is our democracy," he says pointing to the overcrowded houses and teeming streets.

The eldest of seven brothers, Mr. Abbas has been working since he was 12 years old. He takes work whenever he can get it as a laborer and makes between $12 and $16 a day.

Almost 3 million Iraqis ages 18 to 22 will be eligible to vote for the first time in parliamentary elections. After cliff-hanging decisions on an election law, turmoil over the disqualification of candidates accused of Baathist [the political party of Saddam] ties, and a backdrop of election-related violence, Iraqis across the country will go to the polls on March 7 [2010].

Young People Are Frustrated

This is the first election held in a fully sovereign Iraq, after the United States relinquished control over security to the Iraqis last June. And it's the first national parliamentary election expected to include large numbers of Sunni Arabs—a major base of Baathist power under Saddam—who largely boycotted the 2005 vote. So it is seen as the first parliamentary vote that has a chance of electing a truly representative government.

This should be an exciting threshold to a new future for young people. But a broad range of interviews reveal that for this generation, born into a decade of trade sanctions and raised in war, there is an overriding sense of frustration, fears about security, and the struggle to find their place in a country still emerging from conflict.

"A lot of [young people] say, 'What would it matter if I *did* vote?'" says Adel Izzedine, director of the Voice of Fallujah. "They don't understand that their choice will define the future of this country."

There is concern that young, educated Iraqis will not vote; and that in the longer term, they will opt out of playing a role in remaking the country, says Abdul-Rizak Kathim, a sports professor at Baghdad University and a parliamentary candidate. His small party, Scientists and National Qualified Professionals, is campaigning on using Iraq's oil wealth and its technical competence to help rebuild Iraq and provide jobs for young people.

"Our mission now is to explain to young people that it's their national duty to go and vote and help write the future of Iraq," says Dr. Kathim.

Entering their teens when the war started, young people here have spent the past seven years surrounded by chaos and insecurity. It's difficult to find any young person who hasn't lost a relative to the war or the ongoing violence—which together have caused at least 30,000 deaths. Many young people in school or university have walked past bodies in the street to get to class or braved gunfire to take exams. The still-frequent explosions that close the roads are a regular excuse for being late.

With the fall of Saddam, they were left with a huge set of expectations that the government will be unlikely to fulfill.

"There are still kidnappings and bombs. Can we go out safely? We can't," says Nisreen Hamad, a physical education major at Baghdad University. "At 8 p.m. everyone is inside the house. If I'm home after 4:30, everyone says to me, 'Why are you late?'"

She intends to vote, but will take her cue about whom to vote for from her father, who seems to be leaning toward Prime Minister Maliki.

Widespread corruption has also fostered a cynicism about the political process that has persuaded many that it's not worth voting.

In the absence of family or tribal pressure to vote, many young people say they simply won't bother. Mr. Abbas, the teenage father in Baghdad's Sadr City, home to 2 million largely disadvantaged Shiites, doesn't plan to vote. The only reason he gets by, he says, is the government food rations still provided to every Iraqi—and even those are haphazardly come by.

Young Iraqis entering the job market have reason to worry. An Iraqi Youth Ministry survey, shows that more than half of young men between 25 and 30 are unemployed. In Saddam's time, young men were channeled, largely unwillingly, into the Army.

Now, "there are armies of jobless people," says Fawzi Akram, a [city of] Kirkuk member of parliament.

In a country with an insurgency fueled by alienation and economic necessity, that has dangerous repercussions.

"According to our figures . . . 95 percent of the terrorists are uneducated and most of them are also jobless," says Mr. Akram.

Under Saddam, university students studied free of charge and were essentially guaranteed secure government jobs. Now, despite Iraq's oil wealth, government ministries are in a budget crisis and there is no large-scale private sector providing jobs.

It's a generation that has perhaps had it the hardest. The youngest were born in the era of sanctions that followed Saddam's 1991 invasion of Kuwait—a decade of severe shortages of medicine and even books; when private e-mail, satellite TV, and cellphones were banned; and when the West—particularly the US—was reviled.

While almost 60 percent of young people believe that terrorists are the main cause of instability, close to 35 percent believe the US occupation is a main reason, according to a survey of 6,500 young people conducted by the Iraqi youth ministry and the United Nations' World Population Fund.

Isolated from the world by 13 years of sanctions and seven more of warfare, this is the first Iraqi generation to undergo a technical revolution so vast it included not just the arrival of the Internet but of commercial television and mobile phones.

Lack of Education Takes a Toll

It's also a generation less well-educated than its parents, and it is increasingly conservative.

In the past five years, according to UN figures, the number of children in primary education has continued to decline. Girls, particularly, drop out in significant numbers with each subsequent school year. A chronically underfunded education system has led to what development experts consider unacceptably low school enrollment.

The decline in education contributes to ignorance about some key issues. The survey showed that the vast majority of young people believe those who are HIV positive should be isolated from the community. Fewer than 8 percent would share a meal with them. About half believe that the Internet is a bad social influence.

"The Iraqi situation in my opinion has moved to the right in the last five years, which means talking about these issues is more difficult," says Luay Shabaneh, of the World Population Fund.

In this country women have traditionally played strong roles in the workplace, but just a little over 50 percent of young people support women working.

Dr. Shabaneh says that despite the perceived differences between regions of Iraq, the survey released in January [2010] found education, job opportunities, and attitudes essentially uniform nationwide. He says that although the semiautonomous Iraqi Kurdistan, in the north, has a thriving economy, years of trade embargoes and inter-Kurdish fighting have held back development there.

"You cannot really distinguish the Kurdish youth from the rest of the country," he says. "Sulaymaniyah [in the north] is similar to Maysan [in the south]. It's truly Iraq."

When it comes to voting though, in Iraqi Kurdistan, young people have helped fuel their own minirevolution. In regional elections in July [2009], a new party challenging the established main Kurdish political blocs that have run the north of Iraq as a semiautonomous state for two decades captured a quarter of the vote, many of them from young voters weary of what they see as corruption and stagnation. In national elections though, Kurds are still expected to vote overwhelmingly for the two main established Kurdish political parties.

The parliament that the March vote will elect is seen as crucial in deciding the fate of areas long disputed between Kurds and Arabs. Despite trying times, there appears to be a residual optimism among a little over half of younger Iraqis. Of those Iraqis ages 15 to 24 surveyed, 57 percent are optimistic about the future. But that figure declines with age.

Young Iraqis Cynical About Government

"When you look at the factual data—their work, unemployment, education . . . you have one story, and when you look at the future, you have another story," says Shabaneh. "That is to say they haven't lost hope, which for me is an important message."

For many young Iraqis, though, it is an optimism tied to the hazy vision of the distant future rather than shorter-term expectations.

That lack of expectations fosters a cynicism that would normally be surprising in young people and is rooted in a feeling that their elected leaders have done nothing for them.

"The problem is that politicians aren't honest in their promises to young people," says Abbas Kathim al-Shimari, the deputy minister of youth. A move by some members of parliament to lower the minimum age for members of parliament from 35 to 30 has gotten little traction.

Security concerns—both financial and physical—are also causing this new generation to reconsider marriage.

"It's better to be single than to get married, because a year or two after they get married the men are either kidnapped or killed or arrested—even until now," says the Fallujah radio host Abdul Kareem, as she toys with the elaborate gold ring on her finger. "A girl gets married and has a child and her husband disappears from her life."

She readily lists examples: Her cousin's husband was killed last year, leaving her with three children. A friend's husband was killed in the 2004 battle for Fallujah—the friend then married her husband's brother, and last month he was kidnapped and is still missing. "She was married to him for a month," says Abdul Kareem.

Like most residents, Abdul Kareem's family fled the city during the battle in 2004. In 2005, they were worried about security, and her brother took the family's identification papers and voted for all of them—she wasn't sure for whom. They are still worried about safety in the coming election.

She hasn't examined the list of candidates. But if she were to vote, she would vote for someone from her province, Anbar, which includes some of the most prominent politicians recently banned from running for office. She believes the reason for the ban—alleged Baathist ties—are just excuses.

In the colleges, an alarming number of students see so little future here that they want to emigrate—a trend that government officials consider a crisis.

"Our young people are leaving the country and it's a very dangerous indicator—it means that basics for a good life are lacking here," says Dr. Shimari, the deputy youth minister.

Psychologist Layla Ahmed al-Noaimi, a professor at the University of Baghdad, says she was surprised by the survey's findings that only 17 percent of young people wanted to leave Iraq.

"A lot of the young people I talk to want to emigrate in any way possible—maybe more than 50 percent," she says. "They have no security, no work, no marriage—this is very difficult for young men."

Officials fear that the combination of overcrowding, lack of jobs, and sense of injustice is pushing young people to extremism or to the fringes of society in its drug underworld.

"Let us be frank," says Shimari, "the spirit of Iraqi youth is broken, and there is disillusionment and disappointment. Their confidence is shaken because of the wars, because of the pressures of threats. This needs our combined efforts."

Common wisdom has it that the scars of the war will take a generation to heal. For many young people here, it could well be the generation after this one.

The 9/11 Attacks Robbed Students of Their Innocence

Deborah Straw

Deborah Straw is an English professor and writing assessment mentor at the Community College of Vermont.

Terrorist attacks on September 11, 2001, significantly affected community college students. Part of a generation that had been spared national tragedy or war, these young people have suffered a loss of innocence, Straw suggests in the following essay. The aftermath of September 11 has been confusing and frightening for students, and as a result their concentration has deteriorated. Straw reports a decline in the quality of the work she has received post-9/11.

Because of events touched off by Sept. 11, [2001,] many classes at my college [Community College of Vermont in Burlington] have been less cohesive and rewarding than usual this semester, and my English Composition I class has been no exception. Each time I enter my classroom, I see a slightly different group of faces looking at me, and I often collect a mixed pile of due and overdue assignments. More students have been drifting in late, no paper in hand, no real excuse or not even coming in at all. Class size has diminished.

The Quality of Schoolwork Has Suffered

The quality of the work I've received this semester has also been decidedly inferior. I am a fair but tough teacher, demanding several drafts of each paper. I don't take "computer failure" or "the dog ate my disk" stories lightly. The quality of

Deborah Straw, "*A Separate Peace* in a Wartime Classroom," *Community College Week*, vol. 14, December 24, 2001, pp. 4–5. Copyright © 2001 Community College Week. Reproduced by permission.

completed work has suffered, as has the pride in work well done. If this were any other time, I would crack down accordingly. But this is a time like no other for these students.

The planes crashing into the World Trade Center directly affected two young men in my two classes this semester. One is an EMT [emergency medical technician] who knew at least twenty-five firefighters or EMTs who perished. The other lost a high-school friend on one of the planes. Several others have friends and relatives who worked in the World Trade Center, from whom they awaited phone calls for hours or days.

Three of my students have written about their feelings of that day, and although two of these papers were quite unfocused, the writing acted as therapy for them to vent frustrations and fears. In mid-November, when I asked my students if they were still stressed, two students looked at me with relief, saying I was the only teacher to even mention the possibility.

I'm not the only one who has noticed the connection. Rebecca Werner, an associate academic dean at my college who currently teaches an archaeology course on-line, has also seen a real downturn in students' commitment. She tells me, "Everyone is in slow motion. For those on the edge anyway, this is the last straw. They can't concentrate." She has also had more students drop [out of class] than usual.

We agree that we have been slightly more relaxed about deadlines this semester. This is not to say that we will pass slackers. Students have to complete the work and meet the course objectives. However, extending a couple of deadlines seems a fair response—"the humane thing to do," as Werner said. This major disaster has rocked our younger students especially hard, and my classes have many of these.

Here are a few comments I have collected from them: "How can anyone be expected to release their minds enough to allow for the concentration necessary to work out a statistical problem or research a writing topic, when so much threatens the life we hold dear?" . . . "In a strange way, it made me more aware of how precious every minute of every day is. Yet, long term goals seem foolish." . . . "I have changed my outlook on everyday life. I find myself worried about what tomorrow might bring." . . .

"Those of us that lost friends and family are still grieving and this makes it difficult to focus on the future when we can't get by the past." . . . "I've noticed that some other students are depressed by it and can't seem to find a way to function correctly again. There's this dark cloud over everyone's head and it doesn't seem to go away."

The dark cloud lingers.

Innocence Shattered

For many students, this is their first national tragedy. Those of us who lived through the 1960s and 1970s have seen so many others—the assassinations of two Kennedys and Martin Luther King Jr., Vietnam and Watergate—that we are no longer so surprised if things start to fall apart.

But this is these young students' first glimpse that this country may not be the best place in the world. Their idealism has been shattered. As one of my students wrote, they have suffered "a loss of innocence." They've discovered that America may not be the center of the universe, and even that it may not be No. 1 in everything, as we're taught in history classes. I'm sure young men think about whether the [military] draft will be reinstituted—and what their futures as traditional providers might look like. With the economy taking a downturn, heading into a real recession, and companies laying off workers, they have even less hope than they had a year ago. In my small city of Burlington, Vt., employment ads have decreased to a quarter of what they were two months ago.

Students don't know what to think: They're confused, angry, sad, depressed. One young woman, normally an A student, told me last week that she's been getting B's and that she

The author of this viewpoint, Debra Straw, argues that the pictured terrorist attacks of September 11, 2001, robbed students of their innocence. AP Images.

has been taking depression medication and getting therapy as a direct result of what's been happening in the larger world. These young people now live in fear and uncertainty. Their American Dream seems to have been blown away.

Community college students have always had a lot on their plates. Many of them are not filled with reserves of natural resilience. Most do not come to college with much self-confidence or with high professional aspirations. Many, at least in Vermont, come from broken homes, are the first in their families to attend college, perhaps were abused or have recently overcome a serious drug habit. Some are mentally ill; others have spent a year or two in jail. We have a high percentage of single parents among our student body. The younger students are somewhat different socially and economically, but many of them are paying their own way, living alone and are sometimes estranged from their parents. A large percentage of our students work full time on top of their full course load; they are tired and stressed and they are still quite poor—wages are relatively low in Vermont.

When events like Sept. 11, the ensuing war in Afghanistan and the deadly anthrax mailings[1] come along to complicate their lives, bombarding them with images and words day and night on the TV and radio, it's no wonder that concentration and work habits suffer. Mine have suffered, too. Some days I walk around in a haze; I do my grading a bit less quickly.

As teachers at community colleges, we need to understand and even second-guess our students' lives outside our hallways. They are stressed enough without national emergencies occurring at the beginning of a semester. We need to prepare our students for ongoing academia and/or for the working world, but we need also to understand their current lives. My students have learned much this semester, but not, perhaps, what I've taught them in the classroom. They may not

1. In October 2001, authorities discovered letters containing anthrax spores that were addressed to members of Congress.

remember how to do Modern Language Association citations, or how to begin a literary analysis. What they will retain are images of the planes crashing into the World Trade Center, statistics about anthrax and photos of poor children and veiled women in Afghanistan.

But, of course, I've learned something, too. I've learned that these young people are not so different than I was at their age. Sure, they have more tattoos and are somewhat more cynical. But they hurt, they love their parents and they love their country. It's only when we see our students kindly, as individuals—even when we're annoyed that they're not following our rules—that we can help them. By exercising tough love, we can encourage them to grow. More now than in the past 20 years, we need to remain compassionate. Nothing will be the same for them or for us for a very long time.

Despite the Reality of War, Sports Bring Joy

Steve McKee

Steve McKee is an editor for the Wall Street Journal *and the author of* The Call of the Game.

The September 11 attacks remind McKee of his reading, thirty-five years ago, of A Separate Peace. *In the following essay, he writes that one of the themes of the novel—that in the midst of war, simple pleasures can be found in the beauty of athletic endeavor—is highly relevant to him as he anticipates the approach of the 2002 Winter Olympic Games.*

Were you paying attention in 10th-grade English class?

"But the rule that had the most urgent influence in his life was, 'You always win at sports.' This 'you' was collective. Everyone always won at sports. . . . (he) never permitted himself to realize that when you won they lost. That would have destroyed the perfect beauty which was sport."

A Separate Peace Relevant to 9/11 Aftermath

That is from *A Separate Peace* by John Knowles, who died in November [2001] at age 75. His coming-of-age, boarding-school classic was read by all, wasn't it?

I searched out the book soon after Sept. 11, 35 years since Sister St. Cecilia's English class, drawn by what I remembered: Two boys at a boarding school in 1942, one, Phineas (he of the rules) convinces the other, Gene, that there is no war and that there would be an Olympics and it was time to train. Five months before these [2002] Salt Lake City Games, some separate peace, some total denial, wasn't without appeal.

There can't be, of course, and there won't be, as we proceed into this 19th Winter Olympics. Kyoko Ina and John Zimmerman, U.S. medal hopefuls in pairs figure skating, watched the [World Trade Center] towers burn from Hackensack, N.J., near where they train. The U.S. women's hockey team took an especially high hard one: The father of 16-year-old forward Kathleen Kauth was killed at the Trade Center. (Ms. Kauth was left off the final roster; imagine making that decision.) Five members of the U.S. biathlon team, and the armed forces, have stated they would leave immediately if called to active duty. More simply, surely every athlete knows someone who knows someone . . . who didn't come home that night.

"You know where Knowles got his title from, don't you?" Charles L. Terry asked when I called for guidance. Mr. Terry is the Lewis Perry Professor in the Humanities, Emeritus, at Phillips Exeter Academy in New Hampshire, where the author prepped during World War II and later used it as the book's setting, calling it the Devon School. "It's from Ernest Hemingway's *A Farewell to Arms*. Frederic Henry, the narrator, says: 'I have made my separate peace.' Knowles's first title for it was *The Heart in Ignorance*."

It was a terrific read, again, even at age 48. I had forgotten about the tree that Finny falls from (or was he jostled out by Gene?). I had even forgotten that Finny dies. Worse, there was this: There is no such thing as separate peace.

The Olympics Bring Hope amid War

And yet. Isn't it curious that these Games should come here, at this time? Give me the place no one else wants, declared [Mormon leader] Brigham Young, searching for his own sequestration in 1847. No one wanted this place 155 years ago. It was too cold in the winter, too arid in the summer. Now,

The Olympic torch of the 2002 Winter Olympics burns over Salt Lake City, Utah. Author Steve McKee believes the Olympics enforce a theme found in the novel A Separate Peace: *that there is joy in the beauty of the athletic endeavor, even in the midst of war.* © Visions of America, LLC/Alamy.

here comes the world—searching, wondering, hoping, fearing—five months after planes exploded into buildings.

Let's not pretend. The Olympics here are scandal-ridden and politics-driven. And the money! All Olympics are over-commercialized and over-produced. There is too much nationalism, never enough for-its-own-sake competition.

And yet—again and especially now. As Mr. Terry notes: "One thing that Gene says that Phineas says: 'If you love something it will always love you back.' And Gene says: 'Of course, that wasn't true, but like all things Phineas said, it should be true.'" So, too, with these Games. Why not love them?

"Phineas finally does concede that there is a war, much like there is one now," Mr. Terry continues. "But we still want what Phineas wanted. Phineas himself would say it: Look, with all the horror we have to face, the one consolation, the one beauty we can glean from human experience is sport—if people love the Olympics, then there can be an innocence about them, a kind of removal from grim reality."

So forward we stumble, fingers crossed. We should relish this moment with its found opportunity. Tempered by the blast furnace of Sept. 11, we may finally discover that the play itself is the thing [a reference to a line in Shakespeare's *Hamlet*]. It is the athletes alone who can grant us permission to be joyful again. If they exult unencumbered in victory (and despair utterly in defeat), so shall we. But should they wear recent events as a burden, their years of hard work and sacrifice rendered lesser and smaller, not worthy of usual emotion, then we, too, will watch, similarly yoked.

Tonight [February 8, 2002], Salt Lake City's organizers, assorted boosters and moneyed types ignite the Olympic flame for which they paid so dearly. Given the opportunity to bid again on the Games, would they even bother? But they did and here we are.

"Nothing bad ever happens in sports; they were the absolute good," Gene tells us of Finny's rule.

These next two weeks, we'll see.

For Further Discussion

1. In Chapter 1, in a viewpoint written on the twenty-fifth anniversary of the publication of *A Separate Peace*, John Knowles identifies the dualities he was exploring in the novel: "and what was war, and what was aggression, and what were loyalty and rivalry, what were goodness and hate and fear and idealism . . . ?" How are the struggles between these conflicting emotions captured in the personalities of Gene and Finny?

2. In Chapter 2, Simon Raven finds *A Separate Peace* to be a novel espousing pacifism. Do you agree with his interpretation? Cite examples from the novel to support your position.

3. In Chapter 2, Peter Wolfe and James M. Mellard have conflicting views on whether or not Gene reaches his separate peace at the end of the novel. According to Wolfe, Gene's inner struggles outlast the war, and he remains in conflict. In contrast, Mellard sees Gene growing from innocence to maturity in the novel. Which critic do you agree with and why?

4. In Chapter 3, James Palmer describes the experiences of Afghan children who are going to school and growing up in a country torn by war. How are the experiences of these children similar to those of the students at Devon School in *A Separate Peace*? How do they differ?

5. In a viewpoint in Chapter 3, Steve McKee writes that the 2002 Winter Olympic Games brought a welcome distraction and respite to a world stunned by the terrorist attacks of September 11, 2001. He compares the Olympic Games to the events depicted in *A Separate Peace*, where the schoolboys are able to lose themselves in the joy of

competitive sport, thus distancing themselves from the reality of World War II. What role do you feel sports plays in *A Separate Peace*?

For Further Reading

Robert Cormier, *The Chocolate War*. New York: Pantheon Books, 1974.

Stephen Crane, *The Red Badge of Courage*. New York: Appleton, 1895.

Joseph Heller, *Catch-22*. New York: Simon and Schuster, 1961.

John Irving, *A Prayer for Owen Meany*. New York: Morrow, 1989.

James Kirkwood, *Good Times, Bad Times*. New York: Simon and Schuster, 1968.

John Knowles, *Indian Summer*. New York: Random House, 1966.

———, *Morning in Antibes*. New York: Macmillan, 1962.

———, *The Paragon*. New York: Random House, 1971.

———, *Peace Breaks Out*. New York: Holt, Rinehart & Winston, 1981.

———, *The Private Life of Axie Reed*. New York: Dutton, 1986.

———, *Spreading Fires*. New York: Random House, 1974.

———, *A Stolen Past*. New York: Holt, Rinehart & Winston, 1983.

———, *A Vein of Riches*. Boston: Little, Brown, 1978.

J.D. Salinger, *The Catcher in the Rye*. Boston: Little, Brown, 1951.

Tobias Wolff, *Old School*. New York: Knopf, 2003.

Bibliography

Books

Vyvyen Brenden — *Prep School Children: A Class Apart over Two Centuries*. New York: Continuum, 2009.

Hallman Bell Bryant — *Understanding "A Separate Peace."* Westport, CT: Greenwood, 2002.

Sarah Alexander Chase — *Perfectly Prep: Gender Extremes at a New England Prep School*. New York: Oxford University Press, 2008.

Beverly Lyon Clark — *Regendering the School Story: Sassy Sissies and Tattling Tomboys*. New York: Garland, 1996.

Nathaniel Frank — *How the Gay Ban Undermines the Military and Weakens America*. New York: Thomas Dunne Books, 2009.

J. Glenn Gray — *The Warriors: Reflections on Men in Battle*. Lincoln, NE: Bison Books, 1998.

Paul Sackett and Anne Mavor, eds. — *Attitudes, Aptitudes, and Aspirations of American Youth: Implications for Military Recruiting*. Washington, DC: National Academies Press, 2003.

Georges-Michel Sarotte — *Like a Brother, Like a Lover: Male Homosexuality in the American Novel and Theater from Herman Melville to James Baldwin*. Trans. Richard Miller.

Garden City, NY: Anchor/Double-day, 1978.

William M. Tuttle Jr.   *"Daddy's Gone to War": The Second World War in the Lives of America's Children.* New York: Oxford University Press, 1993.

Periodicals

Stephen Armstrong   "Britain's Child Army," *New Statesman*, February 5, 2007.

Hallman Bell Bryant   "Phineas's Pink Shirt in John Knowles' *A Separate Peace*," *Notes on Contemporary Literature*, November 1984.

John K. Crabbe   "On the Playing Fields of Devon," *English Journal*, February 1963.

Joseph Devine   "The Truth About *A Separate Peace*," *English Journal*, April 1969.

Anne Duchene   "*A Separate Peace*," *Guardian* (Manchester), May 1, 1959.

Milton P. Foster   "Levels of Meaning in *A Separate Peace*," *English Record*, April 1968.

Franziska Lynne Greiling   "The Theme of Freedom in *A Separate Peace*," *English Journal*, December 1967.

Granville Hicks   "*A Separate Peace*," *Saturday Review*, March 5, 1960.

William H.
Honan

"John Knowles, 75, Novelist Who Wrote *A Separate Peace*," obituary, *New York Times*, December 1, 2001.

Harding Lemay

"Two Boys and a War Within," *New York Herald Tribune Book Review*, March 6, 1960.

Jorge Mariscal

"The Poverty Draft: Do Military Recruiters Disproportionately Target Communities of Color and the Poor?" *Sojourners Magazine*, June 2007.

Walter R.
McDonald

"Heroes Never Learn Irony in *A Separate Peace*," *Iowa English Bulletin Yearbook*, vol. 22, 1972.

James Holt
McGavran

"Fear's Echo and Unhinged Joy: Crossing Homosocial Boundaries in *A Separate Peace*," *Children's Literature*, vol. 30, 2002.

Marvin
Mengeling

"*A Separate Peace*: Meaning and Myth," *English Journal*, December 1969.

Kathy Piehl

"Gene Forrester and Tom Brown: *A Separate Peace* as School Story," *Children's Literature in Education*, Summer 1983.

W. Michael Reed

"*A Separate Peace*: A Novel Worth Teaching," *Virginia English Bulletin*, vol. 36, no. 2, 1986.

Maurice
Richardson

"*A Separate Peace*," *New Statesman*, May 2, 1959.

| Gordon E. Slethaug | "The Play of the Double in *A Separate Peace*," *Canadian Review of American Studies*, Fall 1984. |

Ronald Weber — "Narrative Method in *A Separate Peace*," *Studies in Short Fiction*, Fall 1965.

Paul Witherington — "*A Separate Peace*: A Study in Structural Ambiguity," *English Journal*, December 1965.

Graeme Zielinski — "John Knowles; Author of *A Separate Peace*," obituary, *Washington Post*, December 1, 2001.

Internet Sources

Azadeh Shahshahani and Tim Franzen — "Military Must Back Off Its Recruitment of Teens," *Atlanta Journal Constitution*, February 10, 2010. www.ajc.com.

Index